D0923160

RING ROUND THE MOON

JEAN ANOUILH

RING ROUND THE MOON

A Charade with Music

Translated by

CHRISTOPHER FRY

With a preface by
PETER BROOK

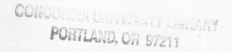

METHUEN & CO. LTD. LONDON
36 Essex Street, Strand, W.C.2

First published May 18th 1950
Second Edition August 1950
Third Edition 1950

CATALOGUE NO. 5314/U

PRINTED IN GREAT BRITAIN
TONBRIDGE PRINTERS LTD., PEACH HALL WORKS, TONBRIDGE, KENT

PREFACE

By Peter Brook

WHEN I saw *L'Invitation au Château* in Paris, I had an appointment at midnight in the Champs-Elysées. The curtain, of course, had gone up very late, the intervals seemed interminable, and long before the last act I had to slip away. The performance on the whole was uninspired, yet the fragment I saw was tantalizing, there seemed an enchanting mood hidden away behind it, and I was in a fever for a copy of the script.

The next morning, again in the Champs-Elysées, I ran into Bébé Bérard. He was shuffling along in his slippers, his beard tucked into his open-necked shirt like a scarf. "Have you seen *L'Invitation au Château*?" I asked. Bérard sighed. "Ah," he said, "what a chance for a designer. . . ."

Thank God, Oliver Messel felt the same thing. But that's to anticipate. To put on a foreign play in London, it's not enough to have read it—though I did the next day—nor to have a management interested—Tennents' were more than interested—nor to have a wonderful designer, nor a lot of actors. All these things are nothing, they neither exist, nor have any chance of existing, without an adaptation of the play that recaptures its quality in English.

This matter of adaptation is one of our greatest nightmares. Although Shakespeare is almost improved in German, and Chekhov is wonderful in French, our language is somehow as insular as our people, and it fights viciously against translators. Every season, plays successful abroad fail in London, their flops have a monotonous regularity, and although the cause is at times the producer or the cast,

5

mostly it is in the change of language. When a play is written in a realistic style, the problem is acute but not insuperable. It is then a question of finding the conversational equivalent, the parallel idiom, colloquialism for colloquialism, slang for slang. But Anouilh is a stylist, he has a manner and a way of phrasing in which much of his charm lies. To translate Anouilh is no matter of matching chat with chat: it demands re-creation, a re-shaping of ideas into phrases that have an English elegance and grace.

This recapturing of a French style has been achieved hardly more than a handful of times in English literature. Molière and Racine have defied a thousand adaptations. Only Otway, perhaps, in a century when for a brief moment English speech and manners approached those of France— in his hardly known translations of *Bérénice* and *Les Fourberies de Scapin*—succeeded.

I approached the task of getting Anouilh recaptured in English with trepidation. When, a few years ago, we had wanted to do Sartre's *Huis Clos*, we had had to reject eight translations. We were in final despair when suddenly the skies opened and a ninth appeared, which was brilliant, and the answer to all our prayers.

Christopher Fry drove us to final despair. He seemed the ideal person for the job. He was already clearly the best word-juggler of all. Also, he had shown proof of his abilities by a piece of nonsense he had translated, in *Twopence Coloured*. Although it only lasted the few instants that a revue sketch is allowed, it was artificial, witty and completely French. But—such is the way of things and writers— Christopher Fry said "No." He read the play, was interested, but none the less, was too hard at work. Entreaties did not move him. Fry appreciated Anouilh, but preferred to observe Venus. So, many months passed with any prospect of staging *L'Invitation au Château* growing fainter and

6

fainter. No other writer was right for this particular play. Then, once again the skies opened, the *deus ex machina* appeared. Christopher Fry, having finished the first act of *Venus Observed*, got stuck. He discovered he didn't know what happened next. It's curious to think how much can hinge on an accident, how this edition, the success of *Ring Round the Moon*, the livelihood of its whole company, and perhaps even the final shape of *Venus*, all owe themselves to this sudden impediment in a muse's flow.

I remember sitting with Fry on the Roman mound overlooking his Shipton-under-Wychwood cottage, and being told the story of the first act of *Venus Observed*. An observatory. An eclipse. And then what happens? I don't know. Perhaps something in a decaying temple by a lake. A few weeks' change from his own play seemed a wonderful idea, the idea of translating became palatable. *L'Invitation au Château* was saved.

The moment Christopher Fry began work on the script we all breathed more freely. But although the quality of the writing seemed guaranteed, the success of Anouilh's play was still much in the balance. Anouilh writes plays for performance rather than for paper. His literary quality is that of theatre literature, the elegance of his dialogue appears when it is spoken by comedians in the rhythm of a comic scene. His first play, *Le Bal des Voleurs*, was called a comédie-ballet, and he conceives his plays as ballets, as patterns of movement, as pretexts for actor's performances. Unlike so many present-day playwrights who are the descendants of a literary school, and whose plays are animated novels, Anouilh is in the tradition of the *commedia dell' arte*. His plays are recorded improvisations. Like Chopin, he preconceives the accidental and calls it an impromptu. He is a poet, but not a poet of words: he is a poet of words-acted, of scenes-set, of players-performing.

7

When the scenery was designed, the actors at work, the scenes beginning to come to life, we realized that an English audience might have difficulty in catching the style of the play. After all, the *commedia dell' arte* is little known here, the idiom is unfamiliar. We had to find a sub-title to make it all clear. But what? A comedy? A farce? A ballet? They all had the wrong connotations. Then Fry found the answer. "Call it a 'Charade with Music'" he suggested. So the reader, too, would do worse than to keep this description in mind, and read this play with sense of theatre and imagination alert. The written play is Anouilh's shorthand for a play performed, and the reader should try to animate the characters until he has them playing and dancing round the ferns and under the twinkling lights of a winter garden. The reader must be his own producer and stage his own charade. Believe me, it's an enchanting game.

This play was first presented at the Globe Theatre, London, by Tennent Productions Ltd. (*in association with the Arts Council of Great Britain*) on January 26th, 1950, with the following cast:

JOSHUA, *a crumbling butler*	DAVID HORNE
HUGO, *a young man about town*	PAUL SCOFIELD
FREDERIC, *his brother, in love with*	PAUL SCOFIELD
DIANA MESSERSCHMANN, *engaged to Frederic, secretly in love with Hugo*	AUDREY FILDES
LADY INDIA, *Messerschmann's mistress, secretly in love with*	MARJORIE STEWART
PATRICE BOMBELLES, *Messerschmann's secretive secretary*	RICHARD WATTIS
MADAME DESMERMORTES, *Aunt to Hugo, Frederic and Lady India*	MARGARET RUTHERFORD
CAPULAT, *her faded companion*	DAPHNE NEWTON
MESSERSCHMANN, *Diana's father, a melancholy millionaire*	CECIL TROUNCER
ROMAINVILLE, *a lepidopterist, patron of*	WILLIAM MERVYN
ISABELLE, *a ballet dancer*	CLAIRE BLOOM
HER MOTHER, *a teacher of the pianoforte*	MONA WASHBOURNE
A GENERAL	MAYNE LYNTON
FOOTMEN	RICHARD SCOTT
	DAVID PHETHEAN

SCENE

The play takes place in a winter-garden, in spring

9

ACT ONE

SCENE 1

A rococo winter-garden; glass and wrought-iron; yellow plush
curtains and green plants. It looks out on to a wide
expanse of park. (Enter JOSHUA, *a butler, and* HUGO,
a young man-about-town, smoking a fat cigar.)

HUGO. And how about last night, Joshua? Did the same
thing happen?

JOSHUA. I'm sorry I can't deny it, Mr. Hugo, but the same
thing did.

HUGO. My brother slept all night under her window?

JOSHUA. Yes, Mr. Hugo—under both her windows. For
five nights now Mr. Frederic has gone to bed in a rhodo-
dendron bush: you know, sir, the one on the south side
of the west wing, beside that statue they call Calliope, a
classical character, sir. Every morning the housemaid has
found his bed unrumpled, and the gardener has found the
rhododendrons rumpled. Well, it gives them a jolt, Mr.
Hugo, as who wouldn't it? I try to make light of it, so as
to keep them in the dark: but one day they'll talk and
Madam will know all about it.

HUGO. Have you ever been in love, Joshua?

JOSHUA. Now, sir, think: I've been in service with Madam
for thirty years; I'm too old.

HUGO. But before that?

JOSHUA. I was too young.

HUGO. Mine's the age for it, Joshua. I fall in love as a
matter of routine. But not ludicrously like my brother.

11

JOSHUA. No, sir. Mr. Frederic hasn't your style at all, sir.

HUGO. And yet we're the same age. It's odd, isn't it?

JOSHUA. You're ten minutes older, sir, remember that.

HUGO. Yes, I know. But who would have thought that those ten minutes would have taught me so much about women?

JOSHUA. The young lady knows she can do what she likes with your brother, sir.

HUGO. She may think she knows. But—I've schemed a scheme.

JOSHUA. I'm glad to hear that, Mr. Hugo.

HUGO. I got up early this morning because I've decided to take action. This dawn is the dawn of the unexpected. What's the time?

JOSHUA. Twelve o'clock, Mr. Hugo.

HUGO. By twelve-thirty, Joshua, I shall begin to loom big on the horizon.

JOSHUA. Oh, and Mr. Hugo, sir—I attempted to explain away the rhododendrons, sir, by informing the gardener that a wolf had been observed making depredations in the vicinity, sir. I told him not to mention this, sir, on the grounds that it might occasion the guests a measure of comprehensible alarm, sir. . . . Thank you, sir.

Exit HUGO. *Enter* FREDERIC. *It is the same actor.*

FREDERIC. Joshua!

JOSHUA. Mr. Frederic?

FREDERIC. Has Miss Diana come down yet?

JOSHUA. Not yet, Mr. Frederic.

FREDERIC. Do I look tired, Joshua?

JOSHUA. If I may be allowed to be frank, yes, you do, sir.

FREDERIC. But you're quite mistaken, you know. I've never slept better.

12

JOSHUA. I think I ought to tell you, sir, the gardener's intending to set wolf-traps in the rhododendrons.

FREDERIC. Never mind, Joshua. I'll sleep in the azaleas.

JOSHUA. And the housemaid, sir, the one who looks after the west wing, she has been making remarks of horrified dissatisfaction. She came to see me quite ready to drop.

FREDERIC. Tell her, next time, to drop into my bed, if she would be so good, and untidy it herself.

JOSHUA. Oh, Mr. Frederic!

FREDERIC. Why not? She's very charming. And when she's unmade it sufficiently she will be able to make it again, and everything will seem to be just as usual.

JOSHUA. Very good, Mr. Frederic.

Exit JOSHUA. *Enter* DIANA.

FREDERIC. Diana! How good to see you again. It's been like a lifetime since yesterday.

DIANA (*stopping and looking at him*). Which one of you is it now?

FREDERIC (*reproachfully*). Oh, Diana; that's not a nice thing to ask me!

DIANA. Ah yes, it is you. You're looking at me like a little lost dog again. Did you get up on the wrong side of the rhododendrons? At first you looked so triumphant I thought you were your brother.

FREDERIC. If you prefer him to me, I shall go away and die.

DIANA. Dear Frederic! You know I should only mistake you by accident. You're so alike.

FREDERIC. Our hearts aren't alike.

DIANA. No, that's true. But imagine me alone in the park one evening: I hear the twigs cracking behind me and

13

what sounds like your step: two arms go round me, and they feel like your arms: a mouth kisses me, and it feels like your mouth. How am I to have time to make sure it's the right heart, Frederic?

FREDERIC. But, Diana, I've never put my arms round you in the park.

DIANA. Are you sure?

FREDERIC. Perfectly sure. Diana! It was my brother, looking like me on purpose! It was my double, double-crossing me again! I must find him: I've got to speak to him!

DIANA (*laughing and stopping him*). Now, dear, dear, *dear, dear, dear* Frederic! Don't go rushing to conclusions. I made it up. No one's been kissing me.

FREDERIC (*hanging his head*). I beg your pardon, Diana. I completely believe you. But if Hugo loved you, I should kill myself.

DIANA. That would be terrible. I should never be sure which of you was dead. (*She is pensive a moment.*) Of course it would be a great help to your brother; he would only have to drop a few tears for you at the funeral, and then come and whisper in my ear, "Ssh: don't tell anyone! They've made a great mistake. This is really Hugo's funeral!" How should I answer that?

FREDERIC. But you couldn't be deceived for a moment, could you? If I were so exactly like Hugo, in word and thought and deed, I should *be* Hugo.

DIANA. Yes, that's true.

FREDERIC (*after a pause*). Diana, it's Hugo you love! Good-bye.

DIANA. Are you mad? I hate him. Kiss me.

FREDERIC (*lost*). Diana!

DIANA. Kiss me, you lost dog, and I'll find your way home for you.

14

FREDERIC. I love you.

DIANA. I love you, too, Frederic.

They kiss.

I suppose you're quite sure you're not Hugo? He's capable of absolutely anything.

They go.

Enter LADY INDIA *and* PATRICE BOMBELLES.

PATRICE. Anything! Anything! He's capable of absolutely anything.

LADY INDIA. But, dear heart, how could he suspect us? We've been so careful.

PATRICE. I tell you, I wouldn't trust that fellow Hugo an inch. Yesterday he giggled at me. Quite noticeably, as I went past him. Why should he have giggled if he didn't know all about us?

LADY INDIA. When did he giggle?

PATRICE. Last night, on the terrace, after dinner.

LADY INDIA. Last night? We were all there together. He choked himself with cigar smoke. He was coughing.

PATRICE. He was coughing to disguise his giggle, but that didn't deceive me for a moment.

LADY INDIA. Anyway, why should this young man, who has nothing to do with me, giggle because he's found out we're having an affair?

PATRICE. Never mind why; mistrust him. To begin with there's this fantastic likeness to his brother.

LADY INDIA. He can't help that.

PATRICE. My dear Dorothy! If he had any sense of propriety, he would never allow it to go on. He revels in it; he copies his brother's clothes.

LADY INDIA. No, dear, Frederic copies his.

PATRICE. Well, it's the same thing. Now, I have eight brothers——

15

LADY INDIA. And they all look exactly like you?

PATRICE. Not at all.

LADY INDIA. I see; then it doesn't help to convince me that this boy would say anything to Messerschmann.

PATRICE. *Say* anything, no; but little jokes and innuendoes when we're all in the drawing-room, yes; a mysterious chuckle in the middle of a meal, or a giggle like the one you thought was choking him with cigar-smoke; yes, most certainly.

LADY INDIA. Little jokes and chuckles will pass right over Messerschmann's head. He suffers from terribly poor reception.

PATRICE. It's we who would have a poor reception if once he knew. Don't forget, you're his mistress and I'm his private secretary. We're both completely dependent on your magnate.

LADY INDIA (*reproachfully*). Dearest heart, you use the most curious words.

PATRICE. Magnate?

LADY INDIA. No.

PATRICE. Private secretary?

LADY INDIA. No. (*She leans against him.*) Patrice, darling, I know I give him the pleasure of paying my bills, and every night I let him trail along to my room to kiss my hand; but that means nothing, and you mean everything.

PATRICE (*desperately*). Dorothy! We're in the winter-garden——

LADY INDIA. On a lovely spring morning.

PATRICE. The season is immaterial! All this glass! Everyone can see us! We're completely exposed.

LADY INDIA. Danger! Oh, that's wonderful; I love it; I like being mad more than anything. Did I ever tell you about the evening in Monte Carlo when I went to a little

16

dockside café, absolutely naked except for a cloak and my diamonds? Quite alone, too, amongst all those drunken brutes.

PATRICE. At Monte Carlo?

LADY INDIA. A little café where the croupiers used to sip a secret Bock between sessions. I just smiled to see how their hands shook when they raised their glasses. . . . So let him come, let him catch us, let him murder us! I shall drive him off with a lash of contempt! . . . It will be magnificent!

PATRICE. Yes.

LADY INDIA. Don't forget you belong to a most distinguished family, Patrice, and I, after all, am Lady India. He should be very grateful that we take the trouble to infuriate him. Money isn't everything.

They go.

Enter MME. DESMERMORTES, *in a wheel-chair, pushed by her companion,* CAPULAT, *and* HUGO.

MME. DESMER. Money is nothing! Oodles, oodles, oodles? Whatever do you mean, Hugo, that Mr. Messerschmann has oodles?

HUGO. He's as rich as Crœsus.

MME. DESMER. Oh, I see—but whatever does he do with it all?

HUGO. Eats noodles.

MME. DESMER. You're being absolutely too playful, Hugo.

HUGO. It's quite true. At every meal, without butter or salt, and drinks water.

MME. DESMER. How very spectacular. And you tell me that Dorothy India is ruining him?

HUGO. She would be, if anyone could be, but there's too much of it even for her.

MME. DESMER (*remembering* CAPULAT). You're a scandal-monger, Hugo. You forget I'm your aunt, and India's aunt. I won't listen to you. I'm an elderly woman, and I never listen to anyone. Capulat, go and look for my handkerchief.

CAPULAT *exits.*

Now, between ourselves, do you really imagine he's keeping her?

HUGO. Between ourselves, without a shadow of doubt.

MME. DESMER. It's monstrous, Hugo; humiliating.

HUGO. Utterly monstrous, but, between ourselves, why humiliating?

MME. DESMER. She is a FitzHenry! And through me, a Desmermortes. If only your uncle Antony were alive it would kill him. Hugo, people are so unkind; they will think I invited Dorothy and this nabob at the same time on purpose. They'll say I'm a party to it. So should I.

HUGO. Everyone knows you invited Mr. Messerschmann and his daughter because Frederic asked you to. Frederic is going to announce his engagement to Diana tomorrow.

MME. DESMER. Yes. There's another puppy-witted piece of folly! Fancy becoming so infatuated with that girl he even has to ask her to marry him! When he was little he always looked so sad and resigned when he came to kiss me on Christmas morning. I used to call him St. Pancras. And now the poor lamb's to be sacrificed. Can you bear to think of him being delivered over, gagged and bound, in his morning coat and gardenia, to this Diana Messerschmann and her millions?

HUGO. No, Aunt.

MME. DESMER. No, I should think not. If it had been you, it would have been different. I love it when the lamb

18

turns round and eats up the high priest. But with poor little Frederic it won't even be funny.

HUGO. If the marriage takes place, Aunt.

MME. DESMER (*with a sigh*). And who can prevent it now?

HUGO. Who knows who?

CAPULAT *returns.*

CAPULAT. Here is your handkerchief, madam.

MME. DESMER. Thank you, my dear. Trundle me into the sun, if you will.

Enter MESSERSCHMANN *and* ROMAINVILLE.

Good morning, dear Romainville! Good morning, Mr. Messerschmann. Have you had a good night's rest?

MESSER. I never sleep, madam.

MME. DESMER. Neither do I. We must make an appointment with one another some time, and gossip while the rest of them snore. We can say the most terrible things about them; it will help to kill time. He takes such a lot of killing, that animal, don't you think? I'm a wicked person, Mr. Messerschmann. Are you?

MESSER. I told you so, madam.

MME. DESMER. How nice. We can be wicked together. That will amuse me very much. Push, dear, trundle me away. I told you I wanted to be in the sun. Oh, Mr. Messerschmann, my butler tells me you only eat noodles?

MESSER. That is so, without butter and without salt.

MME. DESMER. And I believe you're a great friend of my niece, Dorothy?

MESSER. Yes, I have the pleasure of Lady India's friendship.

MME. DESMER. Insomnia, Dorothy, and nothing but noodles! What a *very* interesting life . . .

They go.

ROMAINVILLE *tries to escape to avoid* HUGO.

19

HUGO (*catching him*). Her train gets in at twelve-thirty.

ROMAINVILLE. No!

HUGO. It certainly does.

ROMAINVILLE. I'm convinced it's all a great mistake. It's making me ill with nerves. Are you sure you're not mad?

HUGO. Quite sure. How about you?

ROMAINVILLE. Not at all sure. Suppose I don't co-operate?

HUGO. A scandal, Romainville.

ROMAINVILLE (*losing his temper*). What scandal, for God's sake? My relationship with this girl is absolutely irreproachable.

HUGO. Suppose I say to my aunt, "Our dear Romainville, feeling the approach of springtime in the air, and in order to make his visit to you a cheerful one, has fetched his little friend over to stay at the inn at St. Fleur: he goes to see her secretly three times a week." What do you say then?

ROMAINVILLE. That it isn't true! That I'm only interested in this girl as I'm interested in butterflies and old furniture. Is it my fault if I'm known as a patron of the arts?

HUGO. No.

ROMAINVILLE. The child needed a holiday before she goes back into the ballet. She was rather pale—do understand that, Hugo—she was extremely pale. Anybody would have done the same thing. It's entirely a question of common humanity. I said to her: Come and spend a few days at Auvergne with your mother. Who, for God's sake, is going to make trouble because I give a holiday to a poor girl who needs one? Certainly not your good Aunt, who buttonholes me every year for her local charities.

HUGO. To a poor girl who needs a holiday, no. But to your mistress, Romainville—well, you know my Aunt.

ROMAINVILLE. For God's sake, she isn't my mistress! I assure you she isn't, not the least bit.

HUGO. Who's going to believe you?

ROMAINVILLE. Everybody—because it's true.

HUGO. That's no help. It doesn't seem likely.

ROMAINVILLE. So according to you the truth means nothing.

HUGO. Nothing, dear boy, if no one believes it.

The sound of a dinner gong.

Let's go amiably in to lunch. They'll be here any minute now. I've warned Joshua and he'll let me know. I shall come out and have a word with them, and then, during coffee, Joshua can tell my Aunt that your niece has arrived.

ROMAINVILLE. But suppose my real niece comes on the same train?

HUGO. That's all right. I sent her a telegram from you; you told her that my Aunt's invitation had been cancelled for the time being.

ROMAINVILLE. It's a trap! And all because you found me drinking an innocent orangeade with this little girl, in a cakeshop at St. Fleur!

HUGO. Exactly.

ROMAINVILLE. You're the devil!

HUGO. Almost.

ROMAINVILLE. Would you just tell me what you're up to?

HUGO. A huge and dark design.

The gong sounds again.

There's the second gong. So in to luncheon, Romainville. You shall know everything before you're much older.

They go.

The stage is empty for a moment, then JOSHUA *shows in* ISABELLE *and her* MOTHER *with their suitcases.*

JOSHUA. If the ladies would be so good as to take a seat, I will go and inform Mr. Hugo of their arrival.
He exits.

THE MOTHER. Isn't it luxurious, Isabelle? Such taste! Such grandeur! Now this is the kind of atmosphere where I really feel myself.

ISABELLE. Yes, Mother.

THE MOTHER. Some people, you know, can only breathe where there's beauty and luxury. Take luxury away from them and they go quite limp.

ISABELLE. Yes, Mother.

THE MOTHER. Always remember, Isabelle, your grandfather was the biggest wallpaper dealer in the town. We've even had two servants at the same time, not counting the shop-assistants, of course. When I was your age your grandmother would never have let me go out alone.

ISABELLE. No, Mother.

THE MOTHER. No. The maid always followed three steps behind me. Three steps. It was wonderful.

ISABELLE. Yes, Mother.

THE MOTHER. Did you see the butler?

ISABELLE. Yes, Mother.

THE MOTHER. That dignity, that sort of quilted voice, extremely polite but also slightly scornful, such a perfect manner. (*She mimics him, delightedly.*) "If the ladies would be so good as to take a seat." "To take a seat!" You see how beautifully he chose his words! . . . You know, dear, in my dreams of you, there's always a butler like that in the background.

ISABELLE. Oh, Mother, you know it's not——

THE MOTHER. Ah yes, there is. It's been a dream of mine that you shall have everything I've missed. I don't say very much, I know, but there are times when I suffer. For instance, when I see your hands getting rough and red from washing-up . . .

ISABELLE. Now, please, Mother——

THE MOTHER. I know it means nothing to you, because you haven't my sensitive nature. And I know I don't help you as much as I should. If only I were a little stronger; but even so I have to think of my art, I have to preserve my hands for my piano. And then I never knew what it was to want for anything when I was a girl, so different from you, my poor child, so I mustn't expect you to understand me. You roll up your sleeves, you sing something, and abracadabra everything's done; you think no more about it.

ISABELLE. It's the best way, Mother.

THE MOTHER. I admire you for it. But with my upbringing, and all my dreams which came to nothing, I could never do it. I still have dreams, but now they're for you, Isabelle: a quite different future for you, a future of luxury and beauty, with a little corner somewhere for your Mother. You're artistic, you're pretty, a little more commonplace than I was, perhaps—that's owing to your Father—but interesting and attractive. You will certainly please someone, I'm sure you will. What do you suppose the young man wants you here for?

Enter HUGO.

HUGO. Thank you for being so punctual.

THE MOTHER. Not at all. Punctuality is the politeness of princes, I always think. And I'm sure you'll agree with me.

HUGO. Oh yes, indeed. And this is Miss Isabelle? . . . I wasn't mistaken.

THE MOTHER. She's a charming child.

HUGO. More than charming.

23

THE MOTHER. Mr. Romainville must have spoken about her to you.

HUGO (*not taking his eyes from* ISABELLE). He has indeed.

THE MOTHER. He is one of our dear Parisian friends.

HUGO (*rather coldly*). Yes, I know. How do you feel about this adventure, Miss Isabelle? The most essential thing is for you to enjoy it.

THE MOTHER. She is thrilled about it!

ISABELLE. All Mr. Romainville said was that you had asked us up to your house this evening.

HUGO. Nothing else?

ISABELLE. No, nothing.

THE MOTHER. I expect our friend meant it all to be a surprise.

HUGO. And why should you think I would ask you to come here?

ISABELLE. I don't know. To dance, I expect. I am a dancer.

HUGO. Not only to dance.

THE MOTHER. Not only to dance? Now you're beginning to make me really inquisitive.

HUGO. There's a ball being held in this house tonight. I need you here to be very beautiful, more beautiful, indeed, than anyone else.

ISABELLE. I?

HUGO. Yes. Are you afraid?

ISABELLE. A little. I'm not very beautiful, and so I wonder——

HUGO. I rang up Paris this morning. Roeseda Soeurs are sending some dresses to choose from, and their best fitters. At the first note of the violins, you will be ready.

ISABELLE. But what am I supposed to do?

HUGO. Only to go serenely through the night like a butter-fly venturing on moonlight. With the first light of day we'll set you free. (*To* THE MOTHER.) The engagement will be paid for in the usual way, and the dress will be hers.

THE MOTHER (*simpering*).   Oh, but we didn't think for one moment——

HUGO.   But I thought. Now I must go back to the dining-room or they'll begin to wonder where I am. I'm sorry I can't make it less of a mystery for you. Here is Joshua to show you to your rooms. He will bring you your lunch. No one must know you're in the house. As soon as I can I shall come and tell you what I want you to do.

He goes.

JOSHUA *takes the suitcases.*

JOSHUA.   If the ladies will be so good as to follow me.

THE MOTHER.   Thank you very much. What a distinguished boy, such beautiful manners. Did you not notice, dear, how he kissed my hand? Wake up, dear, are you dreaming?

ISABELLE.   No, Mother. Is he the one they call Hugo? Is he the one who asked us here?

THE MOTHER.   Well, of course. So handsome, don't you think? Now come along, we're keeping the butler waiting. Where are you, my dear, in the moon?

ISABELLE (*in a strange voice, following*).   Yes, Mother.

THE CURTAIN FALLS

SCENE 2

The same scene. The same evening.

MADAME DESMERMORTES *alone.*

MME. DESMER.   Capulat! Capulat! What on earth can she be up to? Capulat! Really, how marooned one is away from a bell-rope. I might be Robinson Crusoe, and

25

without any of his initiative. If only one's governess, when one was a girl, had taught one something practical like running up a flag of distress or firing a gun.

JOSHUA *enters.*

Thank heaven I'm on some sort of navigation route! Joshua! Joshua! ... Ah, Cap Gris-Nez! Joshua! Put into land for a moment, my dear man, and rescue me. I was washed up here fifteen minutes ago, and I haven't seen a living creature since.

JOSHUA. Not one, madam?

MME. DESMER. Not one, and they say the world is over-populated. I sent Mlle. Capulat to fetch the list of guests out of my bureau. You would think I'd asked her to restock the lake with carp, the time it's taking her.

CAPULAT *enters.*

Oh, there you are at last, Capulat. You left me here with a broken brake, and I've had nothing to do but to think over all my shortcomings, *twice.* If you'd been away any longer I should have started to regret them. Where have you been?

CAPULAT. You said the list was in the left-hand bottom drawer, madam, but it was the right-hand top drawer.

MME. DESMER. That's just another way of looking at it. (*She takes the list from* CAPULAT.) Now . . . well, get to work. . . . I must try and remember who all these names belong to. It is so difficult. Nowadays no one has any proper sense of family; people have perfectly good names and then go and produce the most unpredictable faces to go with them. I don't know how they expect to be recognized; and, worse still, it encourages all those terrible people who go to parties without being asked. I remember an evening at the Baroness Grave-Toureau's . . . where is

26

everybody? Capulat, are you listening? . . . I was saying, I remember an evening at the Baroness Grave-Toureau's when . . . well, mend me—mend me! . . . Joshua, I remember an evening at the Baroness Grave-Toureau's when there were so many uninivited guests the Baroness imagined she must be at someone else's party, and spent most of the evening looking for her hostess to say good-bye. Now . . . must you do that? Oh! Deliverance! . . . Now, Joshua, did you hear what I was saying to Capulat? We don't want an unfortunate episode like that. Do you understand, Joshua, we don't want any mistakes.

JOSHUA. Certainly not, madam; though as madam says, faces these days have taken a haphazard turn, most inconsiderate.

MME. DESMER. You will have to look into them very carefully, Joshua, and so shall I. If one stares fixedly at an interloper's frontal bone, fixedly, Joshua, for a count of nine, a look of guilt will steal over it at once. Remember that, Joshua. I intend to stare myself, with great penetration, whenever the occasion offers.

JOSHUA. I hope and trust, madam, that no such occasional offering will ensue. It would be a cloud on an otherwise evening of nice and aristocratic joy, which none of us would like to have to denounce, madam.

MME. DESMER. You're crumbling into a benevolent old man, Joshua. Denouncing—that's delicious; and I depend on you to see that we have no trespassers. Come with me now, and we'll make a last inspection of the battlefield. Well, Capulat, well, my dear.

CAPULAT. I feel so excited, madam, like a little yeasty bun in a good oven, really I do.

MME. DESMER. How splendid! And no doubt the buns feel like little Capulats. . . . Now, the Prince of Palenge, what on earth does he look like, Joshua? Oh, yes, yes, I

27

remember; like a rather half-hearted resolution with a Balaclava beard. . . .

The chair starts suddenly and—

MADAME DESMER MORTES *rolls out followed by* CAPULAT *and* JOSHUA.

After a moment, HUGO *and* ISABELLE *enter.*

HUGO. All right; now just walk a few steps towards me. Turn. Walk away again. You're perfect. What on earth are you trembling for?

ISABELLE. Scared.

HUGO. Scared of what? Of going to a party?

ISABELLE. Yes, I suppose so. The violins tuning up, a house full of strange people all at this moment dressing for the great occasion; and scared of the mystery you're making of it.

HUGO. And scared of me?

ISABELLE. Very much.

HUGO. You think I'm going to drag you into some shameful scene or other. Romainville has been maligning me.

ISABELLE. He said——

HUGO. And of course you believed him?

ISABELLE (*gently*). No.

HUGO. You should have believed him. When you discover what I've planned for this evening, you'll think I'm even worse than Romainville imagines. But you don't have to be afraid of bad people; they're just poor complicated devils like everyone else. It's only the fools who are formidable.

Enter ROMAINVILLE.

And here he is. We were talking about you. How are you this evening?

ROMAINVILLE. Very poorly, very poorly indeed. I'd been looking forward to this party very much, but I feel now

28

as though I were going to an execution. I can't see why you want to go on with it.

HUGO. He's afraid you'll lose your head among the knives and forks, or use a dessert-spoon on the foie-gras, and they'll leap to their feet and say, "This can't be his niece at all! She's an imposter!" . . . Just walk away a little; now turn. Look at that, Romainville. There's a niece for you! Between ourselves, old man, what's your niece really like?

ROMAINVILLE (*stiffly*). She's a rather plain girl. Her nose is perhaps not as small as others. But she has an extremely nice character.

HUGO. It's clearly high time you replaced her. Look at this girl in a dress like the smoke of bonfires. You'll never see a niece more transparent, less of this world, or so entirely fashioned for a singular night of dancing in the early summer.

ROMAINVILLE (*solemnly inspecting her*). Hold yourself upright. When you're presented to people don't address them by their titles. Always wait for an older person to speak to you.

HUGO. Dear me, you're wasting your breath. Isabelle was waiting for older people to speak to her in the womb. My aunt has an infallible instinct for quality, and she's given her a room looking out on to the garden. If she hadn't had the highest opinion of her, she would have put her facing the park.

ROMAINVILLE. Not at all; I'm facing the park.

HUGO (*laughing*). So you see what I mean!

THE MOTHER *enters*.

THE MOTHER. May I come in? May I come in? I couldn't keep away for another minute; I simply had to come and see the dress.

29

HUGO (*going to her, vexed*). I thought it was agreed you should stay in your room. We don't want people asking who you are.

THE MOTHER. I came on tiptoe the whole way; you would have thought I was a shadow. I'm dying of curiosity. Oh, how charming! Oh, how wonderfully elegant! Hold yourself up straight, dear. What good taste! I'm quite sure Mr. Hugo chose it himself.

HUGO. Not at all. Your daughter chose it.

THE MOTHER. Then I'm sure you had something to do with it. Or else the child guessed your taste and chose it to please you.

ISABELLE. Mother!

THE MOTHER. Turn round, dear. Once again. Hold yourself up. She's a constant surprise to me. Dressed, you would think she's *such* a skinnygalee; undressed, she's almost plump. Raspoutini her ballet-master said it's quite simply because she is well-built. As a matter of fact, and I don't say it just because I'm her mother, she has very good legs. This dear gentleman can bear me out, can't you?

ROMAINVILLE (*embarrassed*). Hm! I still thinks she looks extremely pale. We should give her a tonic. That's it, a splendid tonic.

THE MOTHER. Pale! How can you say so? Look at her, she's as pink as a strawberry.

ROMAINVILLE. Hm! The country-air has done some good already, you see. There's nothing like the country, nothing like it.

THE MOTHER. How can you say so? The country is death to her. And to me. We're just hothouse flowers, two Parisians, two artists. In the countryside we just wait to be eaten by sheep. Only our dear friend insisted we should come.

ROMAINVILLE. Her health comes first, her health comes first!

THE MOTHER. Isn't he domineering? His friends must do what he says; he can't bear not to have them with him. When he knew he was coming here, he wouldn't rest until the child came too.

ROMAINVILLE. She looked extremely pale. I said to myself——

THE MOTHER. Yes, yes; and we forgive you because we know you do it out of friendship, just as you did when you made her learn to swim.

ROMAINVILLE (*increasingly embarrassed*). Everybody should learn to swim.

THE MOTHER. He came to the baths himself to watch her, and one day he fell in without taking his clothes off!

ROMAINVILLE (*beside himself*). Didn't I say so, doesn't that prove everybody should learn to swim? We've chattered quite enough; Hugo must be wanting to give Isabelle her instructions. And I know you'd like to see the carriages arriving. You can come up to my room; it faces north, but you can see everyone who comes to the door.

THE MOTHER. Yes, that's it, we'll leave together. Of course I'm burning with curiosity to know what the mystery's about, but Isabelle will tell me tomorrow. Come along, then. I shall hide away like a dilapidated old moth who's been told not to dance round the candles.

ROMAINVILLE (*hurrying her off*). That's right. Like a dilapidated old moth. Off we go. I can hear the first carriages arriving already.

HUGO. And you shall have supper brought up to you.

THE MOTHER. Just a crust, a crust and a glass of water for poor little Cinders. Enjoy yourself, you fortunate girl. I was twenty once; and not so long ago either.... She looks charming, charming!

She goes, dragged off by ROMAINVILLE.

31

HUGO. And she's blushing.

ISABELLE. With embarrassment.

HUGO. Needlessly.

ISABELLE. It's easy enough to talk. My cheeks burn, my eyes are stinging, I've a lump in my throat, and I should like to be dead.

HUGO. She amuses me.

ISABELLE. She might amuse me, too, if only—— (*She stops herself.*)

HUGO. If you had ever listened to what they call a society woman trying to put up the bidding for her daughter, you wouldn't be indignant any more. Your mother's discretion itself.

ISABELLE. I'm not plump, nor a skinnygalee; I've not got very good legs. I don't want to stay here.

HUGO. You can't go yet.

ISABELLE. I feel so ashamed.

HUGO. Why should you be? Because this party and the slight air of mystery has kindled your mother's imagination? Because she likes to think I'm in love with you and tries to throw you at my head? It's most natural. I'm rich, I belong to an old family, and ever since I was marriageable I've heard mothers hammering out that old tune. If you're ashamed because of me, forget your blushes. I've heard the tune so often, I'm deaf to it.

ISABELLE. But I can still hear it.

HUGO. Yes, I can see it must be unpleasant for you. I'm sorry.

ISABELLE (*suddenly*). Have you considered Romainville?

HUGO. Oh no, I never do that. Romainville is scrupulous and considerate, but not considerable. I met you with him in a cakeshop at St. Fleur. I thought you were charming, and it occurred to me you might be very useful this evening. That's all.

ISABELLE.   But I think you should know . . .

HUGO.   I don't want to know anything else at all.

ISABELLE (*softly*, *flatly*).   I see. I only wanted to—to tell
you. . . . Oh dear, I'm silly! I've been crying, and now I
shall have to begin my face all over again. Will you excuse
me for a little while?

HUGO.   Of course.

She goes.

HUGO *signals to* JOSHUA *who is crossing the stage.*

Joshua!

JOSHUA.   Mr. Hugo?

HUGO.   Does anyone suspect anything?

JOSHUA.   No one, sir. The dress-shop people and the shoe-
shop person have went, sir, unobserved. So many outside
individuals here to-night, in any case, making the
preparations. . . .

HUGO.   You'll keep your eye on the Mother.

JOSHUA.   As far as the human eye can be kept, sir.
I beg your pardon, but she escaped my notice just
now. What with all the responsibility for the Ball as well,
sir. . . .

HUGO.   If only she'll content herself with trotting between
here and her room, it may be all right. But she'll
worry me considerably once the evening has really
begun. (*He locks an imaginary door with a key.*) Click,
click!

JOSHUA.   Very good, sir. But if the lady starts to scream?
We have to look all eventualities in the face, sir.

HUGO.   Tell her I told you to shut her in, and promise her
two hundred francs extra.

JOSHUA.   Certainly, sir. . . . Excuse me, sir, but . . . you
think that will be sufficient to—to quench this particular
individual, sir?

HUGO. Quite sufficient.

JOSHUA. Very good, sir.

> *To* ISABELLE *who re-enters*
> *as* JOSHUA *goes.*

HUGO. Everything all right again?

ISABELLE. Yes; no sign of tears now.

HUGO. It's very useful to be able to disappear and come back with new eyes and a fresh smile, ready to pick up the conversation where you left off. The poor naked face of the male has to fight for a façade as best it can. (*He looks at his watch.*) It's almost ten o'clock: your dress makes you look like Helen of Troy: the first carriages are grinding the gravel in the drive: the fiddlers are rubbing rosin on their bows: and it's time I explained things to you.

ISABELLE. High time!

HUGO. I had to get to know you a little first. If you had been a fool I should have thought up a story for you, something picturesque and sentimental, a snip for a housewife's magazine. I'd begun to invent something like that when I asked you to come here. Something conventional; that's always the easiest. But, once in a very great while, something conventional is too threadbare for the circumstances, and a man's left standing stupidly with his intelligence on his arm, like a rolled umbrella he hadn't expected to use. So much the worse for me. Now I shall have to talk without preparation.

ISABELLE. I'm so sorry.

HUGO. Not at all. It's my fault for being such a poor judge of character. I ought to have been able to tell at a glance. You're not a fool, you have simplicity; you're not romantic, you're tender; you're not hard, you're exacting. Each one is almost like the other, but in fact they're opposites.

34

This will teach me to look carelessly at girls in cake-shops!
I'd thought of everything except one. I didn't expect you to
look at me with such penetrating eyes.

ISABELLE. If it upsets you I can shut them.

HUGO. No, it's all right; your penetration will save time.
I can cut the preamble and get to the point. Now, listen.
I have a brother who is addled with love for a rich, young,
beautiful girl. This party is in her honour.

ISABELLE. And she doesn't love him?

HUGO. She's engaged to him, which means that she gives
him her lips two or three times a day, and no doubt lets
him have contact occasionally with her pretty, lukewarm
hand, while she turns her mind to something else. She
makes all the loving gestures expected of her, she even
tells him she loves him, but she doesn't.

ISABELLE. Does she love someone else?

HUGO. I should say she's quite incapable of loving anybody. But as she's a little multi-millionairess, and badly
spoilt, blown skyhigh by every breeze of a whim, she's
made herself believe—yes, that she loves someone else.

ISABELLE. And that person is . . .

HUGO. As you've so quickly guessed, myself. You'll tell
me she must be extremely stupid, because my brother is
at least a thousand times nicer than I am.

ISABELLE. What does he look like?

HUGO. You see, that's the devil of preparing speeches in
advance. I've forgotten to tell you the most important
thing. We're twins.

ISABELLE. You look like each other.

HUGO. Physically, we're so alike it's neither permissible
nor proper. But morally—morally, we're as different as
day and night. My brother is good, sensible, kind, and
intelligent, and I'm the reverse. But nevertheless she loves
me and not him.

35

ISABELLE. And you?

HUGO. I?

ISABELLE. You love her, perhaps?

HUGO. I love nobody. That's why I can organize this evening's little comedy with complete serenity. I'm acting providence tonight. I deflect the influence of the stars! The stars, twinkling up there, without an inkling of what's going to happen tonight. Now this is what I want you to do.

ISABELLE. Tell me.

HUGO. To begin with, unquestioning obedience, and keep your eye on me all the time. I can only give you the broad outline; the details will have to be worked out as the evening goes on. Don't be afraid, you'll never be alone. I shall appear from behind a screen; I shall be behind the sofa where you go to sit with your partner, or under the tablecloth, or lurking in a shadow in the garden. I shall be everywhere, always watching you and whispering my orders to you. It's very simple. All you've got to do is to become the centre of interest; the party must revolve round you and no one else.

ISABELLE. You're expecting too much of me. I can never do it!

HUGO. I can do it. Don't worry, be yourself. Say whatever you want to say. Laugh whenever you want to laugh. If you suddenly feel like being alone, be alone. I shall expound you brilliantly; I shall make everything you say or do seem enchantingly extravagant and witty. I shall make them all think I'm in love with you.

ISABELLE (happily). Will you?

HUGO. And you will make them all think you're in love with my brother.

ISABELLE. But if your brother is in love with this other girl, he won't even look at me!

HUGO. Being a fool, perhaps he won't. But even if he never takes his eyes off Diana *her* eyes will tell him that you're the beauty of the evening. She will be *so* jealous.

ISABELLE. It will make your brother love her more than ever.

HUGO. You think so? What a pretty idea of love you have in the theatre! No, put your mind at rest; I have everything nicely worked out. My brother is going to love you. It's all a question of waking him up. Diana isn't remotely the sort of girl he would want to love. He's suffering in his sleep, walking along a parapet of infatuation, and we're going to waken him.

ISABELLE. Suppose he should die of it?

HUGO. Whoever died of love?

ROMAINVILLE *enters, full spate.*

ROMAINVILLE. There you are, there you are! I've been looking everywhere for you! Catastrophe!

HUGO. What do you mean, catastrophe?

ROMAINVILLE. My dear boy, the whole idea's exploded. Thank God!

HUGO. What are you talking about?

ROMAINVILLE. I was shepherding your mother back to her room, relying on the corridors being fairly dark, and we turned a corner slap into the Capulat!

ISABELLE. Capulat?

ROMAINVILLE. His aunt's companion.

HUGO. Well, you could pass that off all right.

ROMAINVILLE. I passed right on. But what did they do? They threw themselves like a pair of idiots into each other's arms, and burst into tears. It seems that they took piano-lessons together at the Mauberge Conservatoire. They've been thinking each other dead for twenty years, but, astonishing as it may be, they're alive! I was completely helpless. They're there still, looped around each

37

other's necks, telling their life-stories. Thank God they're both talking at once, and neither knows what the other one's talking about. Whatever happens, there's only one thing for it: flight! (*To* ISABELLE) Go up and change. I shall say you've been taken ill, you've had a telegram, your grandmother's had a stroke; I'll say something or other. I've got an imagination too. There's not a minute to lose. Go up and change!

HUGO.   Stay down here. I forbid you to go.

THE MOTHER *knocks and enters.*

THE MOTHER.   Coo-ee! Have you heard *my* little piece of excitement?

HUGO (*going to her*).   Yes. What have you been saying to her?

THE MOTHER.   Oh, my dears, what bliss there can be in a friendship! You've often heard me speak of Geraldine Capulat, haven't you, Isabelle? I thought she was dead: but she's alive, the dear sweet soul. What have I been saying to her? Why, everything, everything, you know: my unhappy marriage, the end of my artistic career: in fact, all my disappointments. You don't *know* what Geraldine has been to me! Both of us with golden hair; we were always taken for sisters.

HUGO.   How did you explain your being in this house?

THE MOTHER.   Quite simply. Did you think I should be taken off my guard? I told her I was one of the orchestra.

HUGO
ROMAINVILLE } Ouf!

THE MOTHER.   But she didn't believe me. It wasn't a fortunate choice. It appears they are all negroes. So then do you know what I did? I have complete confidence in Geraldine. I made her swear on our long friendship that she wouldn't say a word to anybody, and I told her everything.

38

HUGO
ROMAINVILLE $\Big\}$ *(in a panic)*.   Everything?

THE MOTHER.   Everything!

HUGO.   How could you have told her everything? You know nothing about it.

THE MOTHER.   No, but you know I'm quick with my little romances; like a big child, really; I'm incorrigible. I embroidered something to suit the case, a little figment!

ROMAINVILLE.   A little figment?

HUGO.   What little figment?

THE MOTHER.   A little rosy-coloured figment! Oh dear, I believe you're going to scold me.

HUGO.   Let's get to the point: what exactly have you said?

THE MOTHER.   Nothing; just foolishness, words, day-dreams. I said you were in love with my little girl, and you wanted to bring her here without a lot of to-do, so you were pretending she was Mr. Romainville's niece.

ISABELLE *(distressed)*.   What right had you to say so?

ROMAINVILLE.   Good heavens! My dear Hugo, by now your aunt knows the whole thing. I don't know what you're going to do, but I'm leaving. It's a great pity, I shall never be able to come here again. Our whole life gets altered by accidents! Go upstairs and change, for goodness sake!

HUGO *(starting for the door)*.   I shall have to find Capulat. We must make sure she keeps her mouth shut.

At the door he runs into MME. DESMERMORTES *pushed in her wheelchair by* CAPULAT. ROMAINVILLE *and* ISABELLE *hide* THE MOTHER *as well as they can.*

MME. DESMER.   Where are you off to, Hugo, dear?

HUGO.   Nowhere in particular.

MME. DESMER.   Then stop behaving like a cul-de-sac. I've come to see my young guest. Why hide her away in this hole and corner? I congratulate you, my dear friend.

ROMAINVILLE (*with a start, suspiciously*).   Congratulate me? Why congratulate me?

MME. DESMER.   She's very charming.

ROMAINVILLE.   No!

MME. DESMER.   No?

ROMAINVILLE.   Yes!

MME. DESMER.   Is she well and happy?

ROMAINVILLE.   No—not just now. Rather faint.

MME. DESMER.   What nonsense are you talking? Her cheeks are like roses. One dance will put her on top of the world.

ROMAINVILLE (*not knowing what he's saying*).   She's afraid of getting a telegram.

MME. DESMER.   That's a curious anxiety. She's wearing such a pretty dress. Is that your present to her, you generous man?

ROMAINVILLE.   Certainly not!

MME. DESMER.   I hope you like your room, my dear. Tomorrow morning you'll get the very first of the sunshine. Do you mean to enjoy yourself this evening?

ISABELLE.   Oh yes!

MME. DESMER.   Who was it told me it was your first ball?

ROMAINVILLE.   It wasn't I!

MME. DESMER.   Was it you, Hugo? No, it couldn't have been; you don't know her. I hope someone has introduced you?

HUGO.   Yes, Aunt, someone has introduced us.

MME. DESMER.   She's entrancing, isn't she?

HUGO.   Entrancing.

MME. DESMER.   Why don't you ask her to dance? They're playing the first waltz.

HUGO. I was about to. (*To* ISABELLE) Will you give me the pleasure of this waltz, mademoiselle?

They waltz away together. HUGO *drops a word to* ROMAINVILLE *as he goes past him.*

She's bluffing. She doesn't know a thing.

ROMAINVILLE. She knows everything.

MME. DESMER (*watching them go*). She is exquisite, she is pretty, and she's well-bred. How is it, Romainville, you've never talked about her to me?

ROMAINVILLE (*unhappily*). I don't know. . . . I can't explain it at all . . . not even—not even to myself.

MME. DESMER (*signing to* CAPULAT *to push her towards the ball*). Let me think, now: on her mother's side, if my memory serves, she is a Dandinet-Dandaine?

ROMAINVILLE. Yes, but . . .

MME. DESMER. Then she's connected with the Rochemarsouins?

ROMAINVILLE. Perhaps, perhaps, but . . .

MME. DESMER. If she's connected with the Rochemarsouins, she must also be a Cazaubon.

ROMAINVILLE. Yes, I suppose she must, but . . .

MME. DESMER. My poor Antony was a Cazaubon through the Marsusses and the Villevilles, so he would have been as it were a slight relation of hers if he had lived.

ROMAINVILLE. As it were . . . but as it is, he is dead!

MME. DESMER. But I'm still alive, Romainville, and I like to be quite clear about relationships. It's very important I should see exactly how this girl fits in. Now, let me see: you said her mother, who was a Fripont-Minet, is dead.

ROMAINVILLE. Dead!

MME. DESMER. Her mother's cousin, then, one of the Laboulasses. . . .

41

ROMAINVILLE (*interrupting*).   Also dead.

MME. DESMER.   The elder? The one I went to school with? I don't mean the younger one.

ROMAINVILLE.   Dead, dead!

MME. DESMER.   What, both of them?

ROMAINVILLE.   Both of them.

MME. DESMER.   And on her father's side: the Dupont-Pitard family?

ROMAINVILLE.   All dead.

MME. DESMER.   Poor little thing! Why, she's living in a morgue!

ROMAINVILLE.   A charnel-house!

They go.

As CAPULAT *goes she drops her long mauve scarf.* THE MOTHER *comes out of hiding as cautiously as a great mouse. Re-enter* CAPULAT. *She rushes to* THE MOTHER.

CAPULAT.   I told them I had lost my scarf!

They fall into each other's arms.

THE MOTHER.   To see you! To think that I really see you! It's like a dream!

CAPULAT.   It is, isn't it, it really is? The whole thing, the whole thing's such a romance, it really is.

THE MOTHER.   He worships her; you could see it in every look he gave!

CAPULAT.   He's absurdly rich. It really is a romance!

THE MOTHER.   And handsome as a lion! You must help me, my dear, or my little girl will die of it.

CAPULAT.   I'll do anything and everything. The whole thing's such a romance, it really is. Ah, dear! Our little wild whirling days at Mauberge, can you remember them? The cake shop Marius Laubonne!

THE MOTHER.   And the ice creams at Pinteau's!

CAPULAT. And the first duet we played together, at the Charity Concert for the Mauberge Widows' Fund! (*She listens to the music.*) The "Invitation Waltz."

THE MOTHER. The "Invitation Waltz." (*She starts to sing the music.*) La, si, do, re, do, la, sol, la, sol, fa, mi, re, do.

The orchestra takes up the waltz during the final bar and continues playing. THE MOTHER *and* CAPULAT *stand for a moment rocking to and fro, with their heads together, then* CAPULAT *breaks away and creeps furtively off, blowing kisses with her scarf.*

THE MOTHER, *her eyes half closed, her head leaning on her hands, starts to waltz herself.* JOSHUA *appears, moves towards her like a man stalking a butterfly.*

She goes out waltzing without seeing him. He follows her.

THE CURTAIN FALLS ON ACT ONE

43

ACT TWO

Behind the lowered curtain, gay music of the dance.
As the curtain rises, couples are whirling round the stage;
the music comes to an end. and they drift away.
MME. DESMERMORTES *enters in her wheel-chair,*
pushed by CAPULAT.

CAPULAT (*after a pause*). Well, the ball has really got
going now, hasn't it, madam?

MME. DESMER (*peevishly*). It can get going and go, for all
I care. It bores me until I don't know whether to yawn
or yelp. I was never fond of dancing, and since I've been
screwed to this chair, it looks more than ever like the
hopping of kangaroos. You've never liked it either, have
you?

CAPULAT (*simpering*). I was a girl of twenty, you know,
once upon a time.

MME. DESMER. When, for goodness' sake? You've never
looked any different to me.

CAPULAT. Oh yes, I was, madam. I was young when
I was with the Baron and Baroness, before I came
here.

MME. DESMER. Ah, well, you may have thought so.
You're a nice girl, Capulat, but . . . you know this as well
as I do . . . you're plain. No one who is plain can ever
have been twenty.

CAPULAT. But a heart beats in my breast all the same,
madam.

MME. DESMER. My good soul, a heart with no face is
more bother than everything else put together. Let's talk

45

no more about it . . . you've been quite happy, Capulat, without a face; you've been respected, and you've been appreciated. What could be nicer than that?

CAPULAT. On evenings like this, when there's music and the young people dancing under the chandeliers, I feel something indescribable in the air.

MME. DESMER. Then don't attempt to describe it. It's much too late. You really have nothing to grumble about. And there's always the life to come. A dull life in this world is a splendid recommendation for the next.

CAPULAT. Oh, madam.

MME. DESMER. You will be hobnobbing with the Blessed while I'm roasting over a slow fire for two or three thousand years. Well, perhaps it won't seem so long.

CAPULAT. God's mercy is infinite, madam.

MME. DESMER. Certainly; but He must abide by what He says, you know, otherwise the Just like you, who've staked everything on it, are going to feel very badly let down. Suppose a rumour started circulating among the Sheep that the Goats were going to be pardoned as well? They would use such bad language that they'd get themselves damned on the spot. Don't you think it would be rather comic?

CAPULAT. Oh, you can't really think that, madam!

MME. DESMER. Why not? I can think anything I like, it's all I have left to do. . . . Push me nearer the doors where I can see the frisking of little fools. Isn't that Romainville's niece dancing with my nephew?

CAPULAT. Yes, madam.

MME. DESMER. She has a very unusual grace; the only woman who is being herself. Why didn't Romainville bring her here before?

CAPULAT. She's so graceful, really she is, isn't she? She has such . . . what shall I say . . .?

46

MME. DESMER. Whatever you care to, dear; I'm not listening. Do you know what I think? I think you'll need amusing this evening. Now, what can we think of to liven ourselves up?

CAPULAT. A cotillion?

MME. DESMER. A cotillion! That is so like you! You couldn't have suggested anything sillier. Except the ball itself. . . . Look at them twirling and twiddling! They think they're enjoying themselves, but all they're doing is twizzling their vain little heads. The world isn't amusing any more; it's time I left it. The fabulous evenings I've known in my time. In 1902, for instance, at Biarritz, the Duke of Medino-Solar was out-of-this-world in love with the Countess Funela. You won't guess what he did. They were giving a public assembly—a ridotto, it used to be called—and everyone had to be dressed in yellow. Well, the Duke came in green! It was the colour of his mistress's eyes, but of course nobody understood that. The rules of a ridotto were always very strict, and they refused to let him in. The Duke was a Spaniard of the hottest and bluest blood. Without any attempt to explain, he killed the footman. Of course, the ball went on. Their Highnesses the Infantas were there, so it was decided that anonymity should still be respected. The police were brought in, wearing yellow dominoes, and if you happened to dance with them you could see their beady eyes and really horrible moustaches under their masks. But, as they could only dance with the ladies, they weren't able to spot the Duke! The next day he crossed the frontier and a bull killed him in Madrid. That's what living used to be!

CAPULAT. Yes, of course, but one doesn't know, really one doesn't; romantic things may be going on here, at this very moment.

47

MME. DESMER.   At this ball? Dear Capulat, you should go and lie down.

CAPULAT.   Perhaps so, but perhaps not so. Suppose there was a young, rich, handsome man, spellbound with love, who had smuggled his loved one into the ball. . . . But I've said too much. I promised I wouldn't breathe a word.

MME. DESMER.   Why should I suppose there was?

CAPULAT.   And, as well as the young man, an old friend, a dear, dear friend given up for dead, suddenly coming back like the bluebells in May! It's really wonderful, it really is, suddenly to take part in a fairy story!

MME. DESMER.   Bluebells? Fairy story? Capulat, I don't know what you're talking about.

CAPULAT.   To think the world is still so colourful, madam, it really is! Love can still be stronger than social barriers, careless of scandal, as pure as death. There can still be the desperate plot, the impersonation, madam. And the poor apprehensive mother, hiding herself away and watching her child's triumph without ever . . . ever . . . Oh, I really can't stop the tears, madam, I can't really. I'm so sorry!

MME. DESMER.   Suppose you explain yourself, Capulat, instead of watering my hair? What apprehensive mother, what impersonations?

CAPULAT.   Oh, I've said too much! I promised I wouldn't breathe a word!

MME. DESMER.   A word about what?

CAPULAT.   It's a secret, madam; the diamond at the bottom of a mine. She loves him, he worships her, she is poor, he brings her here disguised. It's really like a fairy story, really it is, isn't it?

MME. DESMER.   She? He? Who are these people?

48

CAPULAT. Everyone is either whispering her name or asking who she is. She moves among them like a queen. Her evening of triumph! And her mother played the treble and I played the bass, all those years ago. . . . I'm so sorry; do forgive me; it's all too much!

MME. DESMER. Capulat, you've been my companion for twenty years, and though you've never said anything that amused me I've always been able to understand you. At last you interest me and I can't understand a word. Either you explain, or you leave my service.

CAPULAT. Oh, I've said too much! I promised not to breathe a word. I'd rather die in poverty; I'd rather you killed me!

MME. DESMER. I wouldn't dream of it. I'm used to being obeyed without having to kill people. And you know I always give you my old clothes. Don't I deserve a little consideration?

CAPULAT. I know, I know that, madam! I'm being nearly torn apart by the two duties. Oh, madam, we were such friends, we both played on the same piano! Such happy days! I thought she was dead and I found her again. She told me she belonged to the orchestra, but they were all negroes. I was astonished. Then she confided in me, and swore me to secrecy. All about the mad love of this young man for her daughter, and the stratagem of the good kind friend.

MME. DESMER. What good kind friend?

CAPULAT. M. Guy-Charles Romainville, such a good kind man!

MME. DESMER. What has he done?

CAPULAT. His niece is not his niece. Love snaps its fingers! A young man who is very close to you. But I've said too much. I promised not to breathe a word.

MME. DESMER. Promised whom?

D   49

CAPULAT. My dearest friend. I promised on the days of our duets. So better to die! . . . Oh, madam, the violins! They're like strong wine to me!

MME. DESMER. So I've noticed, mon amie! Push me to my room where we shan't hear them, and tell me the rest of it.

CAPULAT. You're so good, madam; there's nothing you can't do! A word from you, and all the obstacles will evaporate.

MME. DESMER. Well, we shall see about that. Trundle me off and explain things without falling over yourself. You were saying that Romainville's niece . . .

CAPULAT. Is not his niece, madam. She's your nephew's loved one. He wanted her to be the belle of the ball. So he had a dress brought from Paris for her, and he begged her mother, my dear, sweet friend . . .

MME. DESMER. My nephew? Which nephew? Frederic?

CAPULAT. No, madam. Mr. Hugo. But, oh dear, I'm sure I've said too much! I promised not to breathe a word. . . .
They go.

The music wells up again. Enter LADY INDIA *and* PATRICE BOMBELLES, *dancing a Mexican tango.*

PATRICE. They've put me in a room looking out on the park, facing direct north . . . it's most unkind . . . and they've moved all my things, in the middle of the afternoon, without telling me. They said they couldn't find me, but they're not going to make me believe that. I never left the billiard-room. They couldn't find me because they didn't want to find me.

LADY INDIA. Then who has got your room?

PATRICE. Romainville's niece. The girl with the lovely eyes. But that's only the excuse. The real reason is that he saw us together yesterday, and wants to have me further away from your room.

LADY INDIA. Nonsense! He would have to explain it all to my aunt. You mustn't be idiotic. And how do you know she has lovely eyes?

PATRICE. Who, dear heart?

LADY INDIA. This niece of Romainville's.

PATRICE. Have I said so?

LADY INDIA. Now be careful, Patrice. I don't like competitors. And if Messerschmann *has* seen us together and feels like braining you, I shall quite understand. Frankly, Patrice, I should be very disappointed if he didn't. Don't you agree?

PATRICE. Well, I suppose . . . I don't know . . . I suppose so.

LADY INDIA. I may deceive Messerschmann, but I like to think well of him. The man I love must be noble and courageous, and the man I deceive must be noble and courageous too. It gives life a kind of dignity which is most pleasing. Surely, Patrice, you, so proud and susceptible, would be terribly upset if he didn't give a savage cry of uncontrollable jealousy?

PATRICE. I—well, Dorothy, I——

LADY INDIA. Exactly! Men of your calibre wouldn't want a woman who wasn't fiercely loved already. Creatures such as ourselves have no patience with the lukewarm. We blaze! Other people may be born to live, but we're on earth to blaze.

PATRICE. Yes, Dorothy.

LADY INDIA. And it's very nice of us to bother about him at all. Suppose he does ruin us? What fun it would be to be poor, as long as one was *excessively* poor! Anything in excess is most exhilarating.

PATRICE. Yes, Dorothy!

LADY INDIA. Our squalor would seem like a great dark poem, wouldn't it, Patrice?

51

PATRICE.   Very dark!

LADY INDIA.   How amusing it would be! I should wash
the dishes and clean the flues, whatever that may be, and
bake and brew. How beautifully I should brew! I must
ask Roeseda Soeurs to make me some affecting little
aprons. There's no one else, you know, who so well
understands my style. What miracles she will do with a
scrap of muslin and a ruche! And then I shall set to work
with my tiny dustbin and my tiny broom. And you will
work in a factory. I know so many people on the Steel
Board; they'll find you a job as a metal-worker easily.
You will come home in the evening, nearly dead with
fatigue, and smelling dreadfully. It will be absolutely
delicious! And I shall wash you down, my dear, from
head to foot with a tiny sponge. It's beautiful to be poor,
Patrice.

PATRICE.   Beautiful?

LADY INDIA.   Let him come. What is he waiting for? His
money is burning my fingers. I shall give it all back,
immediately, everything except the pearls.

MESSERSCHMANN *enters and stops, not daring to
approach.*

PATRICE (*terrified*).   Do be careful—he's here! Do be
careful!

LADY INDIA.   Don't be such a coward, Patrice!

PATRICE.   I don't like you. I've never liked you. I'm never
likely to like you.

LADY INDIA.   What?

PATRICE.   I'm only with you out of sheer necessity. It's
quite obvious you bore me. Anyone can see that I'm
yawning. (*He yawns.*)

LADY INDIA.   Patrice, don't dare to yawn! Take my arm.
We'll go away, dancing as ostentatiously as possible.

PATRICE. You're crazy!

LADY INDIA. When the bull is drowsy, one stirs it up with a banderilla. (*Aloud, as they dance off.*) Have you ever seen a bull-fight, dear friend?

PATRICE (*aloud*). Yes, dear friend, but I didn't like it.

LADY INDIA (*aside to him*). Hold your head up. Don't look as though we've seen him. He needn't know yet we know he knows.

PATRICE (*stumbling in tongue and foot*). Yes, but perhaps he doesn't know, Dorothy. Don't you think that by seeming to know we know he knows we run the risk of making him know?

They go.

MESSERSCHMANN *makes to follow them. He calls* JOSHUA, *who is crossing the stage.*

MESSER. Come here, my friend!

JOSHUA. Sir?

MESSER. The two people walking along the terrace there; they'd be making for the greenhouses, I suppose?

JOSHUA. Yes, sir. Would you care to give me your order for supper, sir?

MESSER. Noodles.

JOSHUA. Without butter, sir?

MESSER. And without salt.

JOSHUA. Very good, sir.

MESSER (*makes to go, then hesitates*). Tell me, my friend. . . .

JOSHUA. Sir?

MESSER. If I go down those steps, I get to the greenhouses through the orchard, do I not?

JOSHUA. Yes, sir. But if you are hoping to catch up with the lady and gentleman, sir, I take the liberty to say that I've been watching the lady and gentleman, sir, while you were giving me your order, and they've come back into the house by the small door at the end of the terrace. The lady and gentleman have no doubt gone upstairs by the little staircase, sir.

MESSER. I see!

JOSHUA. No doubt they wish to tidy their persons up, as it were, sir.

MESSER (*sighing*). No doubt yes. Thank you.

(*He is going out when* JOSHUA *bows and says:*

JOSHUA. Without butter?

MESSER (*sighing, sombrely*). And without salt.

He goes, JOSHUA *also.*

Couples, waltzing, fill the stage again. FREDERIC *crosses thoughtfully among the crowd of dancers.* ISABELLE *enters. At the end of the dance* FREDERIC *re-enters, still searching, through another door. He sees* ISABELLE. *They stand, looking at one another, a little uncomfortably, on the now empty stage.*

ISABELLE. I hope you'll forgive me?

FREDERIC. For what, mademoiselle?

ISABELLE. I must seem to be following you. I happened to come in here and . . . and found you were here before me.

FREDERIC. Yes, of course.

ISABELLE. I'm enjoying . . . enjoying the evening very much.

FREDERIC. Yes, it's splendid.

A silence. We hear the orchestra playing. They don't know what to say to one another.

That's a very pretty dress you're wearing.

ISABELLE. Yes, it is pretty. (*Another silence, and then she suddenly asks*) Do you believe in them, I wonder?

FREDERIC. Believe in them?

ISABELLE. In ghosts.

FREDERIC. A little. Why?

ISABELLE. You look as though you might be your brother's ghost, made very sad by something.

FREDERIC. It's what I am.

ISABELLE. You're young, you're handsome, and you're rich. What can possibly have made you sad?

FREDERIC. Being handsome, as you call it, being young and rich, and nothing to be gained by it. Will you excuse me if I leave you now?

ISABELLE. Yes, certainly.

FREDERIC *goes into the garden.*

A snatch from the orchestra, perhaps. HUGO *bursts in through another door.*

HUGO. That was perfect!

ISABELLE. I didn't know what to say. I feel very shy with him.

HUGO. Excellent!

ISABELLE. He'll wonder why I'm always at his elbow, and why I keep trying to speak to him.

HUGO. That's what I want.

ISABELLE (*sinking into a chair*). I can't do it any more.

HUGO (*sternly*). We're not yet past midnight, and you have a duty till dawn. Up you get! You're a kindly creature, and this is a kindly action you're doing. I can promise you won't regret it. That's right; look at him just as you're looking now. You're an astonishing actress. Where did you learn that look of deep regard?

ISABELLE. It's my own.

HUGO. Congratulations. Turn it on Frederic from now till morning. He couldn't help being moved by it.

ISABELLE (*softly*). It may be different when it turns on him.

55

HUGO. Well, something in the same line will do. Dear little brother; he's not used to being given pretty looks. Look out, he's coming back. He wants to talk to you after all, you see. Now, compose yourself and use your imagination. I shall be listening.

He disappears.

FREDERIC *returns.*

FREDERIC. My brother was looking for you just now.

ISABELLE. Oh, was he?

FREDERIC. Usually, when my brother is looking for a girl, she knows it.

ISABELLE. Oh. I . . . I didn't know.

FREDERIC. He's very good-looking; don't you think so?

ISABELLE. Yes—very.

FREDERIC. We're as alike as two blades of grass, but it's only men who get us confused. Women always know which is my brother? How do they do it?

ISABELLE. I don't know.

FREDERIC. It's because he doesn't look at them, maybe. That's a very pretty dress you're wearing.

ISABELLE. Isn't it? He's not only good-looking.

FREDERIC. Who?

ISABELLE. Your brother.

FREDERIC. No. He's very intelligent; much more intelligent than I am. Very brave, too; completely fearless; always ready to shoot the rapids or put his hand in the fire. But there's one thing he couldn't ever do, not every day for any length of time. He couldn't be in love; and perhaps that's why they love him. He's very hard, but he's also very kind.

ISABELLE. He's very fond of you. He wouldn't like to see you hurt.

FREDERIC. It would irritate him. It's not so much that

he's very fond of me. It annoys him to see me unhappy. He doesn't like people to be unhappy. Particularly unhappy in love. (*He gets up.*) Honestly, he's looking for you. I'm looking for someone, too. If I come across him during my search shall I tell him where you are?

ISABELLE.   Really, no. Thank you, but don't tell him.

FREDERIC.   He's good company; much more so than I am.

ISABELLE.   I like being with you. Please stay!

FREDERIC *looks at her in astonishment and sits beside her with a sigh.*

FREDERIC.   Oh! How sad it all is!

ISABELLE.   How sad all what is?

FREDERIC.   I'm sorry. What I'm going to say isn't very polite. Perhaps it's impolite, though I don't want to be impolite. But if the girl I'm looking for so unsuccessfully had said what you have just said I might very well have died of happiness.

ISABELLE (*smiling nicely at him*).   Then it's as well that it was I who said it. (*She gets up.*) And it wasn't in the least impolite. I understand how you feel only too well.

FREDERIC (*also rising*).   Thank you for understanding, but forgive me all the same, and forgive me if I go now.

ISABELLE.   Of course.

FREDERIC.   Good-bye.

He goes.

HUGO *enters immediately, by the same door, in a bad temper.*

HUGO.   No, no, no! I didn't bring you here for that!

ISABELLE.   What have I done?

HUGO.   Sighing and hinting that you'd rather be with someone else! No more of that! You're paid to act a part, my dear, so act it. And without being ashamed of it. It's a serious job, and you should try to do it well.

ISABELLE (*gently*). Please don't go on.

HUGO. Why?

ISABELLE. If you went on talking to me in that voice, I should cry.

HUGO. Now that really would be a good idea. I wouldn't have suggested it myself. Manufactured tears always look a bit grotesque; but if you'll cry naturally, excellent! My dear little brother will founder at once!

ISABELLE. Why haven't you a heart?

HUGO. Because my brother has too much. We were born at the same time, and things were divided between us, this and that to me, a heart to him.

ISABELLE. But you must be able to see that I'm unhappy?

HUGO. Splendidly. You have a way of being unhappy that would fetch tears out of a rock. Have you a twin-sister, by any chance, without a heart?

ISABELLE. I can't bear you!

HUGO. It's a very good thing you can't. Tell my brother so, and swim away with him in a flood of sympathy. That's just what I want.

ISABELLE. You don't suppose I'm doing what I'm told this evening just for the sake of this dress and a fee for dancing?

HUGO. My pretty one, I thought nothing so unpleasant.

ISABELLE. I'm not interested in your brother, or in curing him, or in looking well-dressed, or in having everyone looking at me. Men have looked at me before even when I wasn't dressed well. Do you think that's amusing?

HUGO. Don't fight back the tears any more, let yourself go. Cry, cry, cry, my dear. That's better. You see how easy it is.

ISABELLE (*crying*). Now my eyes will be red. Isn't that rather clever of me?

58

HUGO.   Superbly! (*He throws himself suddenly on his knees and declaims theatrically.*)   Ah! Isabelle, dear Isabelle! I suffer too, I die as well!

ISABELLE (*stopping crying*).   What are you doing?

HUGO.   He's coming back. Stay just as you are. I want him to find me at your feet.

ISABELLE.   Oh, no; this is dreadful!

HUGO (*on his knees*).   Yes, my darling. My heart is overflowing! I'm drowning in it! A heart in full flood! Is he coming towards us?

ISABELLE.   Yes. Oh, please get up!

HUGO.   Now's the time; all or nothing. Ah well; I suppose I'd better kiss you.

He takes her in his arms and kisses her. She relaxes with a little cry—then she suddenly asks:

ISABELLE.   Why did you say 'Ah well'?

HUGO (*bowing coldly*).   You must excuse me. A kiss was necessary.

He makes his escape.
She drops to the sofa, crying.

FREDERIC (*entering*).   Are you crying?

ISABELLE.   Yes.

FREDERIC.   You ought to be happy; my brother kissed you. Usually when that happens, the girl is blushing and dancing like fire. But you're pale and you're crying.

ISABELLE.   Yes.

FREDERIC.   I'm sorry. Perhaps he went away because he saw me coming.

ISABELLE.   No.

FREDERIC.   Don't be unhappy. One unhappy person at a party is enough. I don't know how it is, but I should hate it if you were unhappy too.

ISABELLE.   Please let me alone.

FREDERIC.   I want to tell you something; I realize it's no
consolation to hear other people's troubles, but even so.
It's something I've been almost certain about since yesterday. She chose to be engaged to me because she couldn't
be engaged to my brother. She said to herself, "If the other
one won't have me I'll take his double".

ISABELLE.   If that were true it would be shameful.

FREDERIC.   No; very lucky, really. Otherwise she would
never have chosen me at all. Anyway, I'm used to it.
When we were small, if my brother was naughty and the
governess couldn't find him, she punished me. It was a
sort of alternative. Life only comes to me absentmindedly.

ISABELLE.   You, as well.

FREDERIC.   Why do you say "You as well"? You can't
know what it feels like. I don't mean to pay you an empty
compliment, this is hardly the moment; but I'm certain
no one could mistake you for anyone else.

> ISABELLE *is looking off-stage, suddenly tense. She
> shakes her head to someone in the wings.   Then:*

ISABELLE.   It wasn't because of your brother that I was
crying.

FREDERIC.   No?

ISABELLE.   It was because of you.

FREDERIC.   Because of me?

ISABELLE.   Yes—Frederic, it's you I love.

FREDERIC.   Oh!

> *He goes.*

> ISABELLE *runs across the stage;* HUGO *returns,
> dragging her by the hand.*

HUGO.   Very good! But you needn't have run away! That's
the first time anyone has told him they loved him. You

60

see, you've made him walk with quite a swagger! Let's make things even brisker. A pinch of jealousy while the blood's on the simmer. A third young man is in love with you.

ISABELLE. What young man?

HUGO. That's my business; I'll find one. Furious because I never leave your side, he challenges me to fight, and we choose our weapons.

ISABELLE. You're mad!

HUGO. Imagine it—a duel by moonlight, in the spinney, during supper. Conversation disrupted by the sound of pistol shots. They stop the orchestra, and all troop into the park with lanterns and hurricane lamps to look for the corpse. And then you, your wits crazed with love (you do understand you're crazed with love, don't you, Isabelle?)—you throw yourself into the lake. You swim, I imagine? Well, anyway, it doesn't matter; you've got feet, the lake's no depth, and I shall be there. I shall fish you out, carry you back to land, lay you streaming with water on the grass at my brother's feet, and say to him, "There! You did this!" And if he doesn't love you after that he's got more resistance than I have. . . . You're looking rather dubious. Don't you enjoy bathing? I'll treble your fee. I'll buy you another dress. (*He takes her in his arms before she can draw back; he suddenly speaks like a little spoilt boy.*) Be a nice girl, agree to it, to please me. I'm enjoying myself so much tonight, and it's not often that I do.

ISABELLE (*breaking away and running off with the same hurt cry as before*). Oh!

DIANA (*entering suddenly*). Frederic!

HUGO (*turning with a smile*). Hugo, if you please.

DIANA. Oh! I beg your pardon.

HUGO. I'm not blushing. The one who doesn't blush is

Hugo. Remember that: you may find it useful. Are you looking for him?

DIANA. I thought it was Frederic with that girl in his arms. As it was you, it's different. I apologize. Have you seen him?

HUGO. Of course. Everybody except you has seen him. He wanders like a soul in pain through this desert of gaiety. Why? Are you wanting to satisfy yourself that you've well and truly broken his heart this evening?

DIANA. I don't want to break anyone's heart. It wouldn't amuse me. (*She takes a step and stops.*) By the way, when I was in the park yesterday, one of you kissed me, and Frederic swears it wasn't him. I lied so that he shouldn't be upset. But it must have been you. It's the kind of joke I detest.

HUGO. Yesterday? In the park? At what time?

DIANA. Don't pretend not to remember, Hugo. After dinner.

HUGO. After dinner? You've made a mistake, my dear. I was playing billiards with Patrice Bombelles.

DIANA. Frederic swears it wasn't him.

HUGO. I can only suppose it was yet another son of Adam, making the most of some vague resemblance to us.

DIANA. You're wrong to play with your brother's feelings, Hugo; it's too cruel. Even if you loved me, even if your love for me were too strong to control. But it isn't too strong to control, is it?

HUGO. You put me in an impossible situation, Diana. I'm obliged to say No.

DIANA. I hate you!

HUGO. You, as well? I'm not very popular this evening. Have you seen Patrice Bombelles? I gather he's looking everywhere for me. It's funny, but he didn't take to finding me in that little girl's arms, either. It seems he's mad about her. I didn't know, though I suppose I might have guessed, because everybody seems to be. And I admit she's enchanting, and she's wearing a very pretty dress, moreover. Don't you find it so? Well, good-bye. Shall I send Frederic to you?

DIANA. Thank you all the same. I'll find him myself.

He goes.

DIANA *remains alone, unable to relax. Suddenly she calls for her father.*

DIANA. Father!

MESSER. Well, dear?

DIANA. Did you hear him? Did you hear how he was mocking me?

MESSER. No, dear.

DIANA. Why not?

MESSER. Because I wasn't there.

DIANA. Things are going so wrong you'd think we had no money at all. Would you be so good as to make me happy again, at once?

MESSER. But what is the matter, my darling girl? You wanted this boy Frederic and I bought him for you. Is he trying to get out of it?

DIANA. You didn't buy him for me; he loves me. But his brother is laughing at me.

MESSER. I can't give you both of them; not because I'm not rich enough, but it isn't the custom. Marry whichever you prefer.

DIANA. You're not rich enough to buy me the one I prefer. That's why I took the other one.

MESSER. Not rich enough! Don't put me in a rage!

DIANA. Well, look what's happening to me, and it's Hugo who's making it happen, deliberately, I'm certain. I'm certain he brought this girl here, and she's trying to make Frederic lose interest in me; and Hugo, who never looks at anybody, the cold impersonal Hugo, never takes his

63

eyes off her. I should begin to think I wasn't here, except that everyone has such an air of *not* looking at me that I know I must be. It's bad enough to be looked at as though you weren't there, but it's terrible, terrible, *not* to be looked at as though you were. So please set about making me happy again.

MESSER (*thoughtfully*). Who is this girl? I can do almost nothing with a young girl.

DIANA. Romainville's niece.

MESSER. Which is Romainville?

DIANA. He's the one who looks as though he has gone on a horse to catch butterflies.

MESSER. But where does his money come from?

DIANA. He's a director of one of your companies, like all the rest of the men here.

MESSER. What does Romainville seem to be on? Steel, cement, potash, sulphates, zinc, aluminium, creosote, nuts, nickel, emulsion, tyres, bijouterie, sewing machines, tunnels, racquets . . .

DIANA. I think he said something about pig-iron.

MESSER. Pig-iron! Lead me to him. What do you want this Romainville to do, my darling girl? Do you want me to make him send her away at the height of the ball?

DIANA. Oh—do you think you can?

MESSER. I've got them all in the palm of my hand. I lift a finger and their incomes are only half as much.

DIANA. I'm afraid it's impossible, Father.

MESSER (*calmly*). If he has a ha'penny in pig-iron, nothing is impossible.

He takes her by the hand and
They go.

Enter PATRICE *and* HUGO *from opposite sides. The orchestra plays a heroic, warlike tune.*

64

HUGO. Sir?

PATRICE. Sir?

HUGO. I was looking for you.

PATRICE. For me?

HUGO. Yes. I want to speak to you.

PATRICE. About what?

HUGO. You were in the park yesterday, I think, with Lady Dorothy India, my cousin?

PATRICE. Possibly.

HUGO. I noticed you. You seemed to be having a rather heated discussion.

PATRICE. On quite general matters, if I remember.

HUGO. I don't doubt it. But at one moment you must have outgeneralled yourself; the lady slapped your face.

PATRICE. Mine, sir?

HUGO. This one.

PATRICE. You're mistaken, sir.

HUGO. No, sir.

PATRICE. That is to say, the lady may have struck me, but that's no reason for you to think what you appear to be thinking, sir!

HUGO. What do I appear to be thinking?

PATRICE. After all, damn it, a slap on the cheek isn't always the sign of an understanding between a man and a woman.

HUGO. Certainly not.

PATRICE. One slaps the most casual acquaintances, even complete strangers. It proves absolutely nothing. For instance, if I suddenly struck you now, would you deduce from this that we were on amorous terms?

HUGO. I'd protect myself from that to the death!

PATRICE. Then, may I ask, why you're trying to provoke

me? Winks, sighs, hints, unpleasant chuckles, which you try to camouflage with cigar-smoke? You didn't fool me yesterday on the terrace; oh no, I wasn't fooled for a moment.

HUGO. You're very clairvoyant.

PATRICE. I can't go on, I can't go on another hour!

HUGO. This is just what I wanted to make you say. (*He takes his arm.*) Let's talk it over quietly, like the nice fellows we are. I need your help. Between you and me and the bed-post, this long-drawn-out affair with my mad cousin is boring you to desperation—admit it!

PATRICE. I've never said so.

HUGO. Naturally not. But let's speak frankly, shall we? You're in the hell of a cleft stick. If Messerschmann gets to know she's your mistress . . .

PATRICE (*terrified*). Don't say that, don't mention it!

HUGO. He'll break your neck!

PATRICE (*in a terrible state*). I've been enduring this for two years, twenty-four months—a hundred and four nerve-racking weeks, seven hundred and twenty-eight days. . . .

HUGO. Never mind, dear man; it will be all over this evening.

PATRICE. What do you mean?

HUGO. In the simplest possible way. Imagine you're on a visit to the dentist. You've rung the bell, flickered over the pages of the magazines in the waiting-room, and now you're sitting in the dentist's chair. You've shown him the bad tooth; the dentist has seized the forceps. You're a big boy now; it's too late to run off home.

PATRICE. Do you know my dentist?

HUGO. No.

PATRICE. What are you talking about?

HUGO. This! Either you fall in with my plans this

evening, or else, to be honest with you, I make quite sure that your employer knows how you employ yourself.

PATRICE. No!

HUGO. Now I wonder what you mean when you say no?

PATRICE. You're a gentleman, you wouldn't do it.

HUGO. Not by an anonymous letter or by bribing a servant; but though I do things like a gentleman, I do them.

PATRICE. You're contemptible!

HUGO. I see.

PATRICE. And you're not ashamed?

HUGO. Not at all.

PATRICE. Oh. Then there's nothing more to discuss. What do you want me to do?

HUGO. I want you to choose the alternative way of having your neck broken. There's a very charming girl here tonight. It's a matter of the greatest importance, which I can't explain, that you should pretend you're desperately in love with her.

PATRICE. I?

HUGO. You. But that's not all. You've seen me in the arms of this girl, and in a fit of ungovernable jealousy you box my ears.

PATRICE. I?

HUGO. You. Come with me. We put the incident on a proper footing. We fight by moonlight, in the spinney, with pistols. Don't be afraid; I'm a very good shot. I promise I shan't hit you.

They go.

Enter CAPULAT, *followed by* THE MOTHER, *magnificently dressed and plumed.*

67

CAPULAT. Oh! Oh! You look like the best in the land, you do really, really you do!

THE MOTHER. Do I, Capulat?

CAPULAT. Really you do! You couldn't look nicer in that dress if you'd been born in it!

THE MOTHER. It's my dreams come true, isn't it? I feel as if I'd been born in it.

CAPULAT. No one could doubt it. But wait, wait! I'll go and find madam.

As she goes, JOSHUA *enters. He stops suddenly, rooted to the spot, when he sees* THE MOTHER *in her finery.*

JOSHUA. Oh!

THE MOTHER. My man, would you kindly announce me? The Countess Funela.

JOSHUA. The Countess . . .?

THE MOTHER (*magnificently*). Funela!

JOSHUA. (*goes out, shouting*). Mr. Hugo! Help me Mr. Hugo, sir . . .!

JOSHUA *goes out.*
Enter MME. DESMERMORTES, *pushed by* CAPULAT.
JOSHUA *goes past without seeing her.*

MME. DESMER. Where's he running? What is it? Fire? That would be most diverting. . . . Let me see you, ma chérie! Mille tonnerres! Why, she's a great success! Now we'll go in and make a sensation.

Enter HUGO *with* JOSHUA.

My dear Hugo, I know you will be delighted to be presented to one of my oldest and dearest friends. The Countess Funela. We knew one another in Italy. My nephew, Hugo, Countess.

68

THE MOTHER.   I'm so charmed to meet you!

HUGO.   Madam!

MME. DESMER.   Come along, my dear; wheel me, Capulat. I'm so happy to see you again after such a desolation of separation. We can talk about Venice. Such days! Do you remember Palestrini? Such a madman! Jaundice made an end of him. Now I shall introduce you to all my other guests. Tell me, my dear, you have a daughter, isn't that so? What has become of her?

THE MOTHER.   Oh, it's a very long story indeed.

MME. DESMER.   Well, you must let me hear it. We have all the night before us. . . .

   They have gone.

JOSHUA (*badly shaken*).   Here's the key, Mr. Hugo. So she can only have got out through the window, unless madam opened the door herself. The Countess Funela! When she said that, I could have knocked myself down with one of her feathers. (*He so far forgets himself as to sit down and quickly jumps up again.*) Oh, I beg your pardon, sir.

HUGO.   What for?

JOSHUA.   I sat down. Quite an accident, sir. That hasn't happened to me before in thirty years.

ROMAINVILLE (*entering*).   Stop! Oh, stop! Stop!

HUGO.   Stop what?

ROMAINVILLE.   Everything, stop everything! This time it's altogether calamitous! We've fallen into a trap, we're caught by the avalanche! High finance at its worst! Don't say a word about it! Isabelle must be got away this instant, this very moment, or else I'm ruined!

HUGO.   What in the world are you raving about? Everybody's out of their minds tonight!

ROMAINVILLE.   I'm a director of several sulphate companies, and one pig-iron company.

HUGO. Yes, we know that. But what's that got to do with it?

ROMAINVILLE. That's why Isabelle must leave this house at once! Yes: powerful financial interests make it essential! Not a word! I can't explain. Manœuvres at the Stock Exchange. If you won't help me, your aunt can go to the devil. I'd sooner have the scandal. I'd sooner upset her for life. I'd sooner any damn thing! I'm going to tell her the whole truth immediately!

HUGO. Tell my aunt? Just take a look at who she's introducing to everybody, in the middle of the ballroom!

ROMAINVILLE. I'm too short-sighted. I can't see at this distance.

HUGO. Put your glasses on; it's worth it.

ROMAINVILLE (*putting them on*). Good heavens! What on earth is she doing? Am I dreaming or is that . . .

HUGO. Yes. The Countess Funela. She used to revolve in the best Italian circles.

ROMAINVILLE. Is this you up to your tricks again?

HUGO. No. But my aunt is up to hers.

ROMAINVILLE. But why?

HUGO. No reason, which is what makes it serious.

PATRICE (*entering aggressively*). Sir!

HUGO (*who has entirely forgotten*). Sir?

PATRICE. This state of affairs cannot go on, and as you refuse to give the girl up——(*He tries to box* HUGO'S *ears.*)

HUGO (*pushing him tetchily away*). No, no, no! Another time! You're being a nuisance! Later on, later on! Come on, Romainville, we've got to go and stop her jumping in the lake.

He goes, dragging ROMAINVILLE *in a flurry after him.*

PATRICE. All right. I'll come back.

He goes, jostled by the couples who fill the stage wildly dancing the polka.

THE CURTAIN FALLS ON ACT TWO

ACT THREE

SCENE I

The same. (ISABELLE *sits in the centre of the stage.* HUGO
walks about.)

ISABELLE. And so?

HUGO. And so it doesn't amuse me any more. And, anyway,
that moronic mother of yours is going to drop every brick
in the hod any moment now. Look at her: cooing and
clucking and crowing, all our feathered friends rolled into
one. She makes me shiver. She told General de Saint-
Mouton that she's the Pope's god-daughter. He's
delighted; he can see his catholicism becoming profitable
at last; he imagines he's Ambassador to the Vatican
already!

ISABELLE. Am I still to throw myself into the lake?

HUGO. That's no good now; think of something better,
and think quickly, or else my respectable undelectable
aunt is quite likely to spoil the whole thing. I know! I've
got it!

ISABELLE. You frighten me when you say that.

HUGO. There's no doubt you're still the attraction of the
evening, in spite of your mother behaving like a circus.
You've made a sensation: distinction, poise, reserve. Even
the dowagers are on your side.

> "What birdwings rocked her cradle, what swift grace
>   Caught her and taught her limbs to move
> Gravely as shadows in a sunlit place,
>   Or branches in a grove?"

I walk behind you, gleaning the whispers, as flattered as if I were an impresario. Your effect on the men needs no comment. But all the mothers with marriageable daughters have shot their lorgnettes at you; and you emerge unscathed! You return triumphant from the underworld of undertones. And the daughters are white with fury. Where Diana fell they tumble after. But all this is only a curtain-raiser, an appetiser, good enough to revive poor Frederic. Now I'm ready for better things! I'm going to start a rumour that you're not Romainville's niece at all, nor can your mother possibly be your mother. Better still, you're the wonderfully wealthy side-issue of a Portuguese princess and an Admiral, an Admiral who wrote Byronic poetry and was drowned at sea (I shall think of one; there must have been several): and this is your coming-out party, incognito. And in the small hours, when my little puffball of a story has been blown sufficiently from mouth to mouth, when my cuckoo-history has laid its eggs in the well-washed ears of all the little ladies, when Diana is withered with jealousy, when my abstracted brother, vaguely flattered by your smiling on him, has begun to look not quite so submissively at his executioner, I shall step from the wings, climb on a chair as though to announce the cotillion, crave silence and say to them more or less: "My lords, ladies and gentlemen, you've been cuckooed!" And, making the most of the confusion, I shall continue: "Dear asses! Tonight has been all a gullery; a fiction, all of it! Conceived, and planned, and carried out to the letter! During these few memorable hours you've been able to see (I shall say, calling on Diana to witness it) into the hearts of these young ladies: the rocks that lie there, the sediment, the dead flowers. . . . And you have also been able to see (and my gesture will light on you) something too like an angel to

74

be true! You've been made dupes of, ladies and gentle-men! What you have called distinction, breeding, poise, are only pretences. This angel, this girl who made your evening dazzle, is a lay-figure hired by me, a poor little ballet dancer from the Opera brought here to play the part. She's not Romainville's niece, and she's not the daughter of any Byronic admiral: she is nothing at all. And no one would have more than barely noticed her if I'd brought her here to do her usual turn. But her turn tonight has been to represent yourselves. I've thrown her amongst you, dressed by your own dressmaker, using the words of your own kind, and this has been enough to knock sideways for a whole evening the prestige of your society beauty. "Vanity, vanity, all is vanity." I hope at least that my brother Frederic now sees the light. As for me, I find you unutterably dreary. I should be glad to have looked my last on the whole lot of you! Tomorrow I set off by the first train to hunt big game in Africa." . . . How do you like that, Isabelle?

ISABELLE (*softly*, *after a pause*).   What happens to me?

HUGO.   You! What do you mean?

ISABELLE.   I mean, what becomes of me?

HUGO.   What do you want to become of you? You go off home, with the present you well deserve, with your mother on your arm and you on Romain-ville's; and you have a nice dress and a happy memory. Nothing more than that ever remains of a night's dancing.

ISABELLE.   You haven't thought I might be ashamed?

HUGO.   Of what? You're a free spirit, and intelligent. You must loathe all these people as much as I do. Together we're going to have a good laugh at them. What better entertainment? You wouldn't want to be *like* them, would you?

75

ISABELLE. No, but . . . give the dress to someone else and let me go home! I'll call my mother; you can send us back to St. Fleur *now*, and I promise no one will hear of me again.

HUGO. Nonsense!

ISABELLE. It may be, but . . . Not in front of your brother, then! Nor in front of you! Not just yet!

HUGO. (*breaking free and going*). Yes, now! This moment!

ISABELLE (*calling after him*). It's wrong to think only of how it's going to amuse you!

HUGO. It's all there's time for, before we laugh on the other side of our graves.

He goes.

ISABELLE *sinks on to the sofa again with a little hurt cry. Enter* DIANA. *She stands for a moment looking at* ISABELLE, *who raises her head and sees her.*

DIANA. It's quite true; you're wearing a most attractive dress.

ISABELLE. Yes, it is.

DIANA. And you're looking beautiful; that's true, too.

ISABELLE. Thank you.

DIANA. Perhaps not perfectly groomed, still a little too close to nature; and certainly not a very good powder, nor a very good perfume.

ISABELLE (*she has got up*). That must be why I find yours a little too good, and you a little too far . . .

DIANA. Well? Too far what?

ISABELLE. From nature.

DIANA. You've managed quite well; but if one hasn't a maid who understands these things it's almost fatal; with the best will in the world one neglects oneself. No woman

76

can tend herself and altogether survive. Do you get up early in the morning?

ISABELLE. Yes.

DIANA. Yes, one can see.

ISABELLE. Do you go late to bed?

DIANA. Yes.

ISABELLE. Yes, one can see.

DIANA. Thank you. Tell me, do you mind very much?

ISABELLE. Mind what?

DIANA. Wearing something you haven't made yourself?

ISABELLE. As a compensation, my eyelashes are my own.

DIANA. Happily for you. You'll need them tomorrow, without the help you get from the dress.

ISABELLE. I take it away with me. It was given me.

DIANA. That's very nice, isn't it? You'll be able to be a beauty all over again. I believe there's going to be a jolly dance on the fourteenth day of July at St. Fleur. You'll turn all the bumpkins' heads. Do you like my dress?

ISABELLE. Yes, it's most beautiful.

DIANA. Would you like it? I shall never wear it again. I hardly ever wear a dress more than once. Besides, I can't really tell myself I like petunia. Tomorrow I shall dine in rose-pink, rather a miracle dress, a harass of little pleats, twenty yards of them. If you come up to my room I'll show it to you. Come and see it; I'm sure it'll give you pleasure.

ISABELLE. No.

DIANA. Why not? Do you envy me? That's one of the sins, you know. (*She goes to her.*) You'd love to be rich, wouldn't you? If this evening were only a true story, and you had as many dresses as I have!

ISABELLE. Naturally.

77

DIANA. But you'll never have more than one, isn't that so? And if I put my foot on your train, in this way, and tug it a little, you'll not even have one.

ISABELLE. Take your foot away!

DIANA. No.

ISABELLE. Take your foot away or else I shall hit you!

DIANA. Don't squirm, you little fury; you'll do some damage!

The dress tears.

ISABELLE (*with a sorrowful cry*). Oh! My dress!

DIANA. You did it yourself. A few tacks, it will still do very nicely for St. Fleur. It's exciting, I expect, to have such a triumphant evening with a borrowed dress on your back. The pity is, it's over so soon. Tomorrow morning you have to pack your cardboard box, and I shall still be here, and that's the difference between us.

ISABELLE (*looks at her without dislike, and suddenly says*): Is it so pleasant to be unpleasant?

DIANA (*changing her tone, sitting and sighing*). No, not at all. But one can't always be pleased.

ISABELLE. Can you be unhappy as well? That's very strange. Why?

DIANA. I have too much money.

ISABELLE. But Frederic loves you.

DIANA. I don't love him. I love Hugo, and he dislikes my money, and I think he's right.

ISABELLE. Become poor, then.

DIANA. Do you think it is so easy?

ISABELLE. I make no effort.

DIANA. You don't know how lucky you are. I suppose this is a lovely party—but all my friends give parties like it. I shall never again know the excitement of being "invited up to the great house"—and that's so sad.

ISABELLE. So sad.

DIANA. I tell you, money is only worth something to the poor!

ISABELLE. Which proves there is something the matter with the world. (*She moves towards* DIANA.) I have been humiliated and hurt this evening, and my only dress has been torn, because I'm one of the poor ones. I'm going to do what the poor ones always do. I'm leaving words for deeds, and asking you to go away.

DIANA. Go away? Do you think you're in your own home, you little adventuress?

ISABELLE. Go and cry over your millions somewhere a long way off! I'm pretty stupid and very ashamed to have spent so many minutes trying to understand you. So now I shall use the arguments of the poor. If you don't go I shall throw you out.

DIANA. Throw me out? Let me see you try!

ISABELLE. You're going to see me try! And as you wouldn't care if I tore your dress, I shall tear your face instead: God has been unusually impartial, giving us one face each.

DIANA. You're a common little slut. Do you think I'm afraid?

ISABELLE. Not yet. But I think you may be.

ISABELLE *leaps on* DIANA. *They fight.*

DIANA. Oh! You'll ruin my hair!

ISABELLE. You have a maid to put it right! What does it matter?

DIANE (*fighting*). I've got claws as well as you!

ISABELLE. Then use them!

They fight. DIANA *suddenly stops and cries out:*

DIANA. I was poor once, myself! When I was ten I fought all the little toughs on the docks at Istamboul!

79

They throw themselves at each other again and roll on
the ground. Enter JOSHUA, *who gives a yell of terror*
when he sees them and—
  goes off shouting for MR. HUGO.
FREDERIC *enters immediately and stands speechless.*
The GIRLS *see him and loose each other.* ISABELLE
rises first, scratched and dishevelled. She goes to
him.

ISABELLE. Well, are you satisfied now? Don't you think
you've had a great success? You wanted entertainment,
and no one can now say you haven't had it. How is this
for your scandal? You stood up on your chair and told
them who I was: or if you haven't yet, you have no need
to. I'm going to show myself to them, looking as I am.
A common little slut, as this lady called me. You can
watch your bit of fun get funnier. They'll have no doubts
about me now; they'll know exactly where I come from!
Do you want me to tell you the climax of the ball? To
begin with, I insult my mother: I pluck her feathers in
front of them all: and I take her away, back to her piano
lessons. Down the wind goes the Countess Funela! Her
father sold wallpaper; he carried the rolls on his back and
a paste-pot in his hand. They used to give him five francs
a time, which kept him happy because it meant he could
buy himself a drink without telling his wife. That's the
poor for you! You wanted to play with them tonight
because you were bored, but you'll see what a mistake it
was, and how right your nurses were when you were little
and told you not to play with the common children in the
park. They don't know how to play, and I haven't played
for one moment since I came here. I've been unhappy:
isn't that vulgar of me? I've been unhappy. And all
because you didn't understand, or wouldn't understand,

80

that I love you. It's because I love you that I've done my best to dazzle them this evening; it's because I love you that I've pretended to love your brother; it's because I love you that I was ready to throw myself in the lake, like a baby and a fool, to finish it all! If I hadn't loved you, and loved you from the moment we met, do you think I should have agreed to be in your mad puppet show? . . . Well, won't you say something? It's tiresome, of course, this poor girl standing here saying she loves you. But please say *something*. You usually say so much. What's the matter?

FREDERIC (*stammering*). But . . . I'm afraid . . . none of this was me.

ISABELLE. What do you mean, not me?

DIANA. Certainly it wasn't. Look at him. He's blushing: it's his brother!

ISABELLE (*suddenly confused*). Oh, I'm so sorry. . . . I'm so very sorry.

FREDERIC. No, no, no. It's I who should be sorry. I should have . . .

DIANA. Come away, Frederic. There's nothing you need say to this girl. Hugo will send Joshua along to pay her, and she can go home.

FREDERIC. Don't talk like that, Diana.

DIANA. You will come with me now, Frederic, at once, or from now on you can stay away from me.

She goes.

FREDERIC. I came to tell you how distressed I am by what you've been made to go through this evening, how unpleasant and cruel I know it has been. May I ask you to accept my most sincere apologies for all the rest of them here?

ISABELLE (*gently*). You must go. If you don't follow her quickly she going to make you very wretched.

FREDERIC (*bowing*). Will you excuse me, then? (*He takes a step.*) Shall I explain to my brother that you've told me you love him?

ISABELLE. No; there's no need.

FREDERIC *makes a sorrowful gesture—and goes.*
THE MOTHER *sweeps in.*

THE MOTHER. Oh, my dear child! Such mortification!

ISABELLE. I was coming to find you.

THE MOTHER (*sinking into a chair*). Everything has collapsed! The young man has gone mad. He got up on to a chair, and said simply terrible things. There must be something really very wrong with his head. It's most unfortunate. If he had only waited for another hour I should have been spending the autumn with a General, a very nice one. But now everybody will turn their backs on me, I know they will.

ISABELLE (*rising*). We're leaving now, Mother. Take off your finery. You have to give your piano lessons again next week.

THE MOTHER. You're quite extraordinary. There's not an ounce of poetry in you. All our brilliant dreams vanish, and you go on as usual. You're so insensitive. He couldn't have loved you, I suppose, and I was so convinced. . . . Well, why, why should he have asked you here if he wasn't in love with you?

ISABELLE. You've talked quite enough. Go and take off your feathers.

THE MOTHER (*going to her*). Now just listen to me. I've had a long conversation with Romainville. All this business this evening has nudged him awake, and he's spoken up at last. You've seen yourself this evening how the high-flown young men behave. Romainville is middle-aged, steady, and a gentleman. He has had his eye on you for a long time, he told me so himself: he knows just what he can expect. He isn't going into it with his eyes shut. So there you are. He'll see we're both taken good care of; moreover, he hasn't actually said, but I know he means, that when he has talked his family round he may even make a promise to marry you. Isn't that a nice surprise, dear?

ISABELLE.   Now go upstairs.

THE MOTHER (*getting up, furious*). All right then; go your own way; never think of me and all I've done for you! Lose a good chance, you stupid little ninny, and lose your looks, too, before they get you anywhere!

MESSERSCHMANN *enters.*

(*Suddenly all smiles*) Oh, I'm so happy to see you! How do you do?

MESSER (*coldly*).   Well, madam.

THE MOTHER.   The Countess Funela. We were introdduced just now, but in such a hub-bub. . . .

MESSER.   Madam, I must ask you to let me have a few moments alone with your daughter.

THE MOTHER.   But of course you may. I give you my permission without any hesitation at all. . . . I'm leaving you with Mr. Messerschmann now, Isabelle. I'm going upstairs for a little rest. These social occasions, you know, are so tiring. One comes to wish for a little peace and quiet. We go out too much, I'm afraid, a great deal too much. I'll leave you. . . . Don't forget about our good friend, Isabelle. We must give him an answer tonight, you know, to his charming invitation for the summer. . . . Dear sir, I'm delighted to have seen you again!

She flounces away.

MESSER (*speaking straight out*).   Now, young lady, I'm going to be rather brutal. I know who you are, and in half an hour's time everybody will know. The party's over, as far as you're concerned. You've had a great success, everybody's been charmed by you, but it was a little adventure which couldn't last. I've come to ask you to cut it even shorter. Go up to your room and disappear without seeing anyone again. And I shall be most grateful to you.

ISABELLE.   How can it affect you whether I go or stay?

MESSER.   It's a little present I should like to give my daughter. You see, I make no bones about it. I've never deceived anyone in my business affairs, and I've always succeeded. How much do you want?

ISABELLE.   Nothing. I had decided to go before you asked me.

MESSER.   I know. But it isn't fair that you should go without being paid. How much did Hugo promise you?

ISABELLE.   My usual dancing fee, and this dress, which someone has torn.

MESSER.   Who tore it?

ISABELLE.   Your daughter.

MESSER.   Then that's my business, too. As well as what you were going to ask me, I'll pay for two more dresses.

ISABELLE.   Thank you, but I'm happy with this one, with the tear.

MESSER.   Let's get the situation clear. I don't want you to see Hugo again, even to get your fee. How much do I pay you to go without seeing him?

ISABELLE.   Nothing at all. I didn't expect to see him.

MESSER.   But how about the money he promised you?

ISABELLE.   I don't intend to take it. I can be said to have danced here this evening for my own pleasure.

MESSERSCHMANN *looks at her for a moment, in silence, then weightily and powerfully moves towards her.*

MESSER. I don't like it when things don't cost anything, young lady.

ISABELLE. Does it disturb you?

MESSER. It's too expensive. Why are you refusing Hugo's money?

ISABELLE. Because I'm glad not to take it.

MESSER. And mine?

ISABELLE. Because you haven't any reason to give it to me. I was asked to act in a comedy here this evening. My performance is over, the curtain is down, and I'm going home.

MESSER. But not with nothing to show for it?

ISABELLE. Why not?

MESSER. It's not as it should be.

ISABELLE. I'm sorry, but it's what I'm going to do. You will excuse me. (*She starts to go.*)

MESSER (*suddenly furious*). No, no, no! Don't be like Ossowitch!

ISABELLE (*stops, astonished*). Like Ossowitch?

MESSER. Yes. He was a banker of a rival group, and I had to have important discussions with him. I never met such a man for getting up and going. Whenever we disagreed, which was pretty often, he got up and went. Every time I had to catch up with him in the vestibule or in the lift or somewhere. And the further I had to go to catch him, the more it cost me. In the end I had to invite him to come out in a canoe, when I'd first made quite sure he couldn't swim. After that we were wonderfully good friends: but now he has learnt to swim and things are not so nice. So don't you start this getting up and going, my dear child, it isn't a good way to talk. Nobody ever agrees with anybody in a business discussion, but we stay sitting, or else business is no good. Now, come along, my dear young lady, be reasonable. Strike a good bargain with me before it's too late. What do you want?

85

ISABELLE. Nothing.

MESSER. It's too much. Now, look, I'm going to be foolish. I'm going to offer you twice what you expect. I've the notes on me here. (*He brings a bundle of notes from his pocket.*) Look at this bundle here, such virgins and so clean, such a pretty little bunch! It would be very nice, you will agree with me, to carry about a sprig or two of these little papers?

ISABELLE. How should I carry them?

MESSER (*suddenly like a shopkeeper*). Would you like me to wrap them up for you? I could make you a nice little parcel of them.

ISABELLE. Listen. I don't want to have to walk out like Mr. Ossowitch; I don't want to bring back unhappy memories to you; but I insist that you believe me. I don't want your money.

MESSER (*pocketing the notes, furious*). You're being very exorbitant.

ISABELLE (*looks at him and says*): Is it really possible to be a great power in the world without being very intelligent?

MESSER. I am intelligent! I'm very intelligent! It's because I'm very intelligent and experienced that I tell you I don't believe you!

ISABELLE (*taking him gently by the arm*). Then, if you're intelligent, let's talk intelligently. If you hadn't kept me here I should have been gone already. So you see I have nothing to sell.

MESSER (*angrily*). There's always something to sell! Anyway, even if you haven't, I've got to buy something now we've started bargaining.

ISABELLE. Why?

MESSER. Why? Because I should lose all faith in myself if I didn't.

86

ISABELLE (*with a slight smile*).   If it takes so little to make you lose faith, I must write to Mr. Ossowitch.

MESSER (*calmer*).   Ossowitch was a baby. But you're an opponent who interests me. What I'm buying from you now isn't my daughter's peace of mind any more, it's my own peace of mind. And I put no limit whatsoever on that. How much do you want?

ISABELLE.   Do men become masters of the world by continually repeating themselves?

MESSER.   You're as rich as any girl in the house tonight. And if I want it, Romainville shall adopt you: you really will be his niece!

ISABELLE.   Thank you.

MESSER.   Listen. I'll make you so rich, the grandest and handsomest young fellow here will ask you to marry him immediately.

ISABELLE.   I'm sorry. But none of that will please me as much as saying No to you.

MESSER (*suddenly howling*).   Whatever shall I do? I don't believe in money any more either! All it gives me is dust, smoke, nausea, and indigestion. I eat noodles and I drink water, and I get no pleasure at all from my frozen snow-queen mistress: I don't even suffer when she deceives me, because I don't really want her: I want nothing at all! I'm a poor little tailor from Cracow, and my only really pleasant memory is the first suit I made when I was sixteen: a jacket for a priest, and it turned out very well. My father said to me: "This time you have done it well: you know now what your calling is." And I was happy ... but since then I've succeeded at nothing, except at making money, more and more money, and money has never made anybody love me, not even my own daughter. Please be sympathetic. Do stand by me this evening. Take my money!

ISABELLE. No.

MESSER. No? Ah well: now you can see what I'll do with these beautiful little bundles which can't do anything: I'll bite them and tear them with my teeth and spit them on the ground!

He has taken the bundle of notes and starts tearing them with his own teeth; then, soon, for the sake of speed, with his hands.

ISABELLE (*joyfully*). What a good idea! Give me some, I'll help you. This will make me feel much better!

She takes some of the bundles and starts happily and quietly tearing them up. They throw the scraps of paper into the air. They both work feverishly in a rain of paper.

MESSER (*in a kind of fury*). There! So! So! There! So! That's a country house: the dream of all the small householders!

ISABELLE (*tearing away merrily*). With the garden, the pond, the goldfish, the roses!

MESSER. Everything! There goes a business. A millinery business: the one I was going to give you, like the fool I was!

ISABELLE (*tearing*). Hooray! That was a hat!

MESSER (*annoyed, but not stopping*). Why only one hat?

ISABELLE. It was very expensive!

MESSER. There go the dresses, and still more dresses, rolls and folds and billows of material, what they're all dying to put on their backs. There go the cloaks and the coats and the wraps and the furs!

ISABELLE (*tearing*). Not too many: it's nearly summertime!

MESSER. Away goes the beautiful linen, the satin sheets, petticoats as light as cobwebs, embroidered handkerchiefs!

ISABELLE (*tearing*). There goes a trunk!

MESSER (*stopping in surprise*). Why a trunk?

ISABELLE. To put everything into!

MESSER (*starting again*). There go the necklaces, the bracelets, the rings—all the rings!

ISABELLE (*tearing*). Oh! Such a beautiful pearl!

MESSER. You'll regret that!

ISABELLE (*taking more to tear*). No, not a bit!

MESSER. Away go the holidays abroad, the servants, the racehorses, the beautiful ladies ready and willing, away go the consciences of honest men, and all the prosperity of this lamentable world! There! There! There! There! (*He tears the last of the notes and turns to her.*) Are you happy now?

ISABELLE (*softly*). No. Are you?

MESSER. Not at all.

They are kneeling side by side, exhausted. ISABELLE *finds one untorn note on the ground and tears it up.*

ISABELLE. There go the poor! We'd forgotten them. (*A pause. She looks at the exhausted* MESSERSCHMANN *and asks him gently*): I bet it wasn't so exhausting to get it all!

MESSER. I'm very unhappy.

ISABELLE (*with a wry smile*). Me, too.

MESSER. I understand very well how you feel. And I'm the only person in this house this evening who does understand. For a long time, such a long time, I was humiliated, until I became stronger than they were. Then I could turn the tables. Every man is quite alone. That's definite. No one can help anyone else: he can only go on.

G 89

They both look straight in front of them, squatting on the ground in the middle of the torn notes. JOSHUA *enters and finds them so, to his surprise.*

(*Seeing him*) What do you want?

JOSHUA. It's Mr. Hugo, sir: he wishes to speak to the young lady in the little drawing-room, to settle her account.

ISABELLE (*getting up*). Tell him he doesn't owe me anything. Mr. Messerschmann has paid me.
She goes.

MESSERSCHMANN *watches her go, then rises with difficulty, with* JOSHUA'S *help.*

MESSER. My friend.

JOSHUA. Sir?

MESSER. You seem to have a pleasant face.

JOSHUA (*after the first astonishment*). I belong to a generation of old servants who could never permit themselves to have such a thing while on duty, sir. But on Sundays, and particularly on holidays, my friends tell me I have an amiable face, sir, almost jovial, what I hope I may call a nice face, very French and very homely, sir.

MESSER. Then listen to me. You must have read your Bible when you were a little boy?

JOSHUA. Here and there, sir, like everybody else.

MESSER. Did you ever come across Samson?

JOSHUA. The gentleman who had his hair cut, sir?

MESSER. Yes; and he was very unhappy. Jeered at, my friend, always jeered at by everybody. They had put his eyes out. They thought he was blind, but I'm sure he could see.

JOSHUA. Quite possible, sir. . . .

MESSER. And then, one fine day, unable to stand it any more, he got them to lead him between the pillars of the temple. He was very strong, terribly strong, you understand? He twined his arms round the pillars . . . (*He puts his arms round the dismayed* JOSHUA.) Like this!

JOSHUA. Oh, sir! Do take care, sir, someone will see us!

MESSER. And then he shook them with all his might. (*He shakes* JOSHUA.)

JOSHUA (*being shaken*). Yes, sir! Do be careful, sir! I'm the one who will get into trouble!

MESSER (*letting him go with a sigh, his feelings relieved*). There!

JOSHUA (*putting himself to rights*). Well, there, sir. (*He adds, for something to say*): It wasn't at all the thing to do in a church. . . .

MESSER (*with a dark chuckle*). You might well say so. He was so strong the entire temple crumbled down on to the two thousand Philistines who were there praying to their false gods, and thinking Samson no better than a fool!

JOSHUA. But it fell on him, too, sir.

MESSER. It fell on him, too. But that wasn't of any kind of importance. How could being poor hurt him!

JOSHUA. If you say so, sir.

A pause. JOSHUA *starts to go.*

MESSER. My friend.

JOSHUA. Sir?

MESSER. I'm putting through an overseas telephone call from my room tonight.

JOSHUA. Certainly, sir.

MESSER. That's all. Like Samson. With my eyes tight shut.

91

JOSHUA (*going*).   Quite so, sir.

MESSER.   And all at once there's a frightful uproar, a telephone ringing in the small hours. And that is the temple starting to crumble. Do you understand?

JOSHUA.   No, sir.

MESSER.   It doesn't matter. (*He finds a forgotten note in his pocket and gives it to* JOSHUA.) Here's a thousand francs. Forget everything I've said. (*As he goes out, he turns and says*): And for supper, you remember . . . without butter.

JOSHUA (*bowing*).   And without salt.

THE CURTAIN FALLS

SCENE 2

As the lights begin to fade in, ISABELLE *is seen wandering across the stage. She drifts across the bridge and away into the park towards the lake.*

MADAME DESMERMORTES *wheels herself in, watching* ISABELLE *through her opera glasses.*

CAPULAT *enters in a terrible state.*

CAPULAT.   Madam, madam! Everyone's searching the place for Isabelle. Her mother is out of her mind!

MME. DESMER.   Why?

CAPULAT.   She has left her ring, the only valuable thing she has, wrapped up in a piece of paper on her dressing-table. Oh, madam, madam, we're all to blame! Mr. Hugo didn't love her!

MME. DESMER.   You can cry later on, Capulat. Look out there, down to the lake; I can't see. Is there a white figure there?

92

CAPULAT. There is, you're quite right. And it's Isabelle, it really is, it is really! Oh dear, oh dear, unhappy girl! Oh, madam, she's leaning over the water. Oh, madam, madam, madam, she has jumped! Rescue her! Rescue her! She'll be drowned, really she will, she will really!

MME. DESMER. No, she won't. Hugo is down there, and there isn't enough water. But she might quite well catch cold, and so might he. Run and get some blankets.

CAPULAT. Mr. Hugo is there, you're quite right, he's there. He has plunged into the water—oh, hero! It's all right, I think, madam, it's all right. He'll save her.

MME. DESMER. It could hardly be less difficult.

CAPULAT. He has picked her up in his arms, he has really, and they're coming glittering across the grass in an armour of moisture, madam, as you might say.

MME. DESMER. As I certainly wouldn't say. Stop talking nonsense, you stupid woman, and go at once and find some blankets.

 CAPULAT *hurries off.*

Joshua! Joshua! Someone! Quickly!

JOSHUA (*appearing*). Madam?

MME. DESMER. I'm afraid we're having a little drama here this evening, Joshua: heartbreak and attempted death by water. I'm so sorry. Do go down to the kitchens and make some very hot punch.

JOSHUA. Yes, madam. Nothing serious, I hope?

MME. DESMER. Not at all. What a blessing you are, Joshua. Do try never to break *your* heart, won't you?

JOSHUA. I handle it with as much care, madam, as if it was yours. It's quite safe with me, madam.

MME. DESMER. The punch, Joshua.

JOSHUA (*bowing*). Hot and very soon, madam.

 As he goes—

Enter HUGO *and* ISABELLE *wrapped in blankets, and followed by* CAPULAT.

CAPULAT. They're safe, madam, they're safe, but they're wet!

MME. DESMER. I can show almost no surprise. Go and tell your friend that her daughter is well.

CAPULAT. I will. She was out of her mind!
    She goes.

MME. DESMER. Are you cold, my dear?

ISABELLE. No, thanks; no, no, I'm not.

MME. DESMER. Joshua has gone to fetch you some punch. Are you cold, Hugo?

HUGO. Frozen, thank you, aunt.

MME. DESMER. Then let's make the most of being alone for a few minutes. Stay as you are. Sit down. Sit down, Hugo. Now, look at me, my dear.

    ISABELLE *looks at her.*

She looks even prettier with her hair down. Why do you ever wear it up?

ISABELLE. It's the usual way.

MME. DESMER. Is it also the usual way, at the first crossing of love, to walk into a lake? You can swim, I imagine?

ISABELLE. Yes, I can swim.

MME. DESMER. You see how absurd you are!

HUGO. I suppose it was my fault. I asked her to pretend to drown herself for love of Frederic; but I cancelled the arrangement immediately afterwards. I simply don't know what she thought she was doing.

MME. DESMER. Why should you want to drown yourself?

ISABELLE. For my own reasons.

HUGO. It wasn't in our agreement. You were supposed to do what you were told.

94

ISABELLE. My working-day was over. You had already sent the butler to pay me; and I think I'm allowed to kill myself in my own free time, if I want to.

MME. DESMER. Certainly she is! And it's very nearly morning, and Sunday morning, too. If a working-man can't kill himself on a Sunday morning we can have the revolution at once.

> "For pity, pretty eyes, surcease
>   To give me war! and grant me peace."

You know you're a madman, don't you, Hugo?

HUGO. Yes, aunt.

MME. DESMER. He doesn't love you, my dear, and he'll never love you. He'll never love anyone, I think, if that's any consolation to you. He'll be amorous, perhaps, like a cat with a mouse, from time to time; but you're too delicate a mouse: he would eat you too soon, which he wouldn't like at all. And I'm going to tell you a splendid thing: he's not your sort of cat, either. You think you're in love with him. In fact, you're not in love with him at all. Look at him. Look at him. Look at this sulky Red Indian. Isn't he comic?

ISABELLE *looks at* HUGO.

You find him so handsome? Well, so he is, tolerably, when he's not thinking of anything. Clear eyes, straight nose, an interesting mouth. But let even the smallest of his wicked little thoughts creep into him—look at him now, for instance: we're irritating him: he wants to strangle us— and the change is quite terrifying. The nose is getting pinched, there's an angry little crease tugging the mouth, the eyes are turning themselves into gimlets. . . . And this chin! It suddenly makes him, wouldn't you say, into a fairly pretty but entirely wicked old woman?

No one's altogether handsome who isn't altogether human.

HUGO (*getting up in a rage*). That's quite enough! If you want to analyze faces I'll go and send Frederic to you.

MME. DESMER. That's a very good idea.

HUGO *goes*.

No, my dear, it's the appearance of Hugo you love, not Hugo.

ISABELLE (*hiding her eyes and crying*). Oh, it's terrible!

MME. DESMER. It would be terrible, if we only had one specimen; but fortunately we have two.

FREDERIC *enters*.

(*To* FREDERIC) Come here, my nephew. You can look at him, Isabelle; it's the same picture as before. Here is a young woman who was going to drown herself, and we can't get her to tell us why.

FREDERIC (*to* ISABELLE). I know why. I wish I could help you, but there's nothing I can do. There's something I want to tell you. When I left you just now I was being a coward for the last time. I followed Diana when she told me to. But when I caught her up I couldn't help telling her how wickedly she had treated you. And it's all over now: our engagement is broken off.

ISABELLE. Oh, no, no! Do you think it does any good for us both to be unhappy at once?

FREDERIC. I don't know, but I do know I couldn't love someone who could be so cruel.

MME. DESMER. Neither can Isabelle. She's beginning to see she could never love Hugo.

FREDERIC. I've finished with love altogether. I saw down to the sea-bed of a woman's heart.

ISABELLE (*smiling gently*). The rocks that lie there, the sediment, the dead flowers, as your brother said.

FREDERIC. It's the worst plunge I ever took.

MME. DESMER. Come up to the surface again; there's still some dry land in places.

FREDERIC. I'm going to find a desert island, out of the way of it all.

MME. DESMER. And so is Isabelle. Make sure that your desert islands aren't too far apart. You can have visiting days, hermit to hermit.

FREDERIC. I could have forgiven her for being unkind . . .

ISABELLE. I saw from the first I had to take him as he was, and forgave him for that, but . . .

FREDERIC. I could have forgiven her for being hard, egotistical and hot-tempered . . .

ISABELLE. I could have forgiven him . . .

MME. DESMER. The only thing you could never forgive them was not loving you. We're terrible tailors! We cut the cloth, take no measurements, and when it doesn't fit we cry for help.

FREDERIC. And no one comes.

MME. DESMER. Or so we think. Not content with being blind we have to be deaf as well. We all go howling along together, never seeing or hearing who's beside us, and then we say we're in a wilderness! Luckily there are certain old women who have begun to see more clearly, just at the time, alas, when they're having to take to spectacles. Didn't you hear anything, young lady? This young gentleman called for help.

ISABELLE. How can I help him?

MME. DESMER. You can take him into the park and tell him why you feel so unhappy. And he'll tell you why his life seems over. Go along; be as sad as you possibly can;

97

give her your arm, Frederic. You're quite alone in the world. No one is more hopeless than you are.

FREDERIC (*going with* ISABELLE). It's my own fault for being such a fool. I imagined women could be warmhearted and have sincerity.

ISABELLE. And, of course, they can't. I imagined men could be honest and good and faithful.

FREDERIC. Faithful! We're faithful to ourselves, that's all. We dance the dance of the heart obstinately in front of a mirror. But I expected the dance to be with a partner.

ISABELLE. And there are no partners . . .

They have gone.

MME. DESMERMORTES *watches them off.*

MME. DESMER. Good. Those two only need another five minutes. Now for the others. (*She calls.*) Hugo!

HUGO *enters by another door.*

HUGO. Yes, Aunt?

MME. DESMER. That's as good as done. Now what have you decided?

HUGO. What do you want me to decide?

MME. DESMER. Either I'm a dense and myopic old woman, my dearest Hugo, or you're in love with Diana, and she with you, and you have been since the first day you met.

HUGO. Absolutely ludicrous! And even if it were true, I'd rather die of jaundice, like your friend Palestrini you were talking about, than give her the pleasure of hearing me say so.

MME. DESMER. You can't die of jaundice—Palestrini's as well as you or I. Only last year he threw himself into a lagoon because he was in love with an Austrian swimming champion. She rescued him, and they have a baby.

Enter PATRICE BOMBELLES.

98

PATRICE. Oh, there you are, I've been looking for you everywhere.

MME. DESMER. What does this madman want?

PATRICE. Sir, as you will not give this young woman up of your own accord . . . (*He slaps* HUGO'S *face.*)

HUGO (*slapping back*). Go away, for heaven's sake. I won't have you making such a confounded nuisance of yourself.

PATRICE. Well, may you be forgiven . . .

HUGO. May I be forgiven. . . . Are you insulting me?

PATRICE. Yes, I am insulting you. You told me to insult you.

HUGO. Well, now I'm telling you to stop insulting me. Go away for goodness sake. . . .

PATRICE. I demand satisfaction. . . .

HUGO. If you don't go I shall knock you down.

PATRICE. The arrangement was pistols—the arrangement was pistols.

HUGO *leaps on* PATRICE. *They fight in spite of* MME. DESMERMORTES *trying to separate them with her stick. Enter* LADY INDIA, *terrified.*

LADY INDIA. Patrice!

PATRICE (*freeing himself at once*). Oh, my goodness, look, she's here! Do try to seem friendly. (*He puts his arm round* HUGO'S *shoulder.*) We were playing, my dear! We love playing together! A little early morning exercise, you know.

LADY INDIA. This is no time to be taking exercise, Patrice! Do you know what has happened? I've had a call from Paris. Messerschmann is out of his mind. He is selling in London, he is selling in New York, he is selling in Paris. He's ruining himself!

99

PATRICE.   I don't believe it. I'll go and ring up his agent!
He rushes out.

DIANA *enters.*

DIANA.   Have you heard the news? Within six hours my father will be a poor man.

HUGO.   What are you going to do about it?

DIANA.   Be poor. What do you expect me to do?

HUGO.   Marry Frederic, who is rich.

DIANA.   I don't want him. And now he doesn't want me. Look at him, down there in the park with the little adventuress. She hasn't lost much time tonight. Was it you, Hugo, who taught her how to find a rich husband in one evening? You will have to teach me. I need one now.

HUGO.   Let's be quite clear about this: it's a lesson that wouldn't help you in the least.

He starts to go. MME. DESMERMORTES *stops him.*

MME. DESMER.   Hugo, where are you going?

HUGO.   I'm going to find Frederic. It's no good his thinking he can break the engagement now. Diana's ruined, and the honourable thing is to make her his wife.

DIANA (*in tears*).   But I don't want him!

HUGO.   We can't help that.

He goes.

MME. DESMER.   Mille tonnerres! He's going to mix everything up again!

Enter CAPULAT *and* THE MOTHER.

CAPULAT.   Madam! News! Extraordinary news! It really is!

MME. DESMER.   I think we have heard it.

THE MOTHER.   You've heard it? Now how could that possibly be? But news travels so fast these days. Here he is, to tell you himself.

100

Wedding March from the orchestra. Enter ROMAIN-
VILLE *in morning coat and white gloves, carrying a
bouquet. He goes to* MME. DESMERMORTES.

ROMAINVILLE.   My dear friend. In the first place, please
excuse my clothes, but as dawn is about to break I
changed into a morning coat: I felt it to be the correct
wear for the present occasion. I'm going to give you some
interesting news: my niece, dear friend, is not my niece—
that was an entirely imaginary relationship spun from
your nephew's fancy. But she is about to become even
more nearly related. After extremely careful thought, I've
decided to marry her.

MME. DESMER.   My good man, I would be the first to
congratulate you, but I have an idea that you're too late.

ROMAINVILLE.   Too late? What can you mean? It's five
o'clock in the morning.

ISABELLE *and* FREDERIC *come in with their arms round
one another.*

MME. DESMER.   (*To* ISABELLE *and* FREDERIC.) Well, my
dears, what news have you for us? Have you altered the
fit of the coat?

ISABELLE.   There wasn't any need to alter it! It fitted
perfectly!

FREDERIC.   Aunt, I must have been out of my mind. I
don't love you any more, Diana; do forgive me.

ISABELLE.   Why couldn't I have known it before? It was
Frederic, just as you said.

MME. DESMER.   Romainville, you'll have to get some
other niece. This is the one you have to give away!

ROMAINVILLE.   It's appalling! I had just begun to like
the idea!

JOSHUA *enters, carrying a tray.*

MME. DESMER (*to* JOSHUA). Joshua, give him some of the punch.

ROMAINVILLE *drinks the punch.*

But where is Hugo? Someone go and find him at once. He has made this girl unhappy for quite long enough. (*To* DIANA.) Don't be too dismayed; he loves you, he told me so.

LADY INDIA. Why, look! He's down there in the park, escaping!

MME. DESMER. Escaping? Joshua, catch him before he goes, and bring him here.

JOSHUA *goes.*

(*To* DIANA.) He's a thoroughly crack-brained boy, but he knows he's cornered; he's certain to come back.

DIANA. But suppose he doesn't love me?

MME. DESMER. Impossible. Everything has to end happily, it's only decent. Besides, here he is. Well, Hugo?

They all look at the door through which HUGO *should come. A pause. It is* JOSHUA *who enters.*

FREDERIC. I knew he wouldn't come!

JOSHUA. Mr. Hugo has given me this note for you, madam.

MME. DESMER. Read it aloud, Joshua.

JOSHUA (*puts on his glasses and reads*). "Dear Aunt,—For reasons which you all know, I'm not able to appear among you to take part in the general rejoicing. There's nothing I've ever regretted more. But now Diana is poor I know I love her. Nothing will separate us again. I shall marry her. Tell her to look for me in the park."

102

MME. DESMER (*to the happy* DIANA).   Off you go!

DIANA.   Yes, I will! Oh, Hugo! Hugo!

> DIANA *goes.*
>
> *Enter* MESSERSCHMANN *with a little overcoat, a little hat, and a little suitcase. Mocking music from the orchestra.*

MME. DESMER.   What's this, will someone tell me?

MESSER.   It is I, madam. I've come to say good bye.

MME. DESMER.   But the suitcase, the hat, the coat?

MESSER.   I borrowed them from your butler. I've nothing of my own to put on. I'm ruined. I shall return them in a few years' time. I'm going back to Cracow, on foot, to start a small tailoring business.

LADY INDIA (*running into his arms*).   Oh, my darling boy, what a great, great man you are after all! You must love me so much, so beautifully. It was for me, wasn't it, that you ruined yourself? I'll follow you: barefooted to the bottom of the Steppes of Siberia!

MME. DESMER (*to the others*).   She gets so muddled.

LADY INDIA.   I'll cook for you, my darling, in your dark, dingy igloo, ever your faithful squaw.

MME. DESMER.   She hasn't even a working idea of geography.

> *A frightful racket suddenly, flashes and bangs. Everybody turns round. Enter* PATRICE BOMBELLES.

PATRICE.   There they go! They've started!

LADY INDIA.   What is it? The fire from heaven already?

MME. DESMER.   No. We haven't deserved that, not quite, not yet. It's my firework display, which all the upset tonight has made a little late. Come along, come and watch: the gardener will be so disappointed if we don't.

It will feel rather odd, in broad daylight. We shall hardly be able to see them.

As they all go out—

Enter JOSHUA *with a telegram. He plucks* MESSERSCHMANN *by the sleeve.*

JOSHUA. Sir, a telegram for you, sir.

MESSER (*opening it*). Who is still sufficiently interested in me to send me a telegram? A letter would have done just as well. (*He reads it and sighs.*) How funny it all is. . . .

JOSHUA (*compassionately*). All over, sir, is it? If you should still need anything, sir . . . I've got a small amount in the savings-bank. . . .

MESSER. What? No, thank you. It's not so easy to ruin yourself as you'd think. It was believed to be a manœuvre on the stock exchange. They bought everything, and now I'm twice as rich as I was before! . . . But I do beg of you: don't let anyone know.

JOSHUA. I must say, I'm very happy for you, sir. I should have felt very sad, sir, not to have brought you your breakfast. (*He has taken up his butler's stance, and says*): Without butter?

MESSER. Yes, my friend. But this morning, as a special celebration, you may add a little salt.

JOSHUA (*following him*). Ah, it's a happy day for me, sir, to see you taking such a pleasure in life again. . . .

They go.

THE CURTAIN FALLS